thinkpink

think pink

mood and colour for modern living

tricia guild

text by elspeth thompson with tricia guild

photographs by james merrell

quadrille

contents

For LL, whose heart is full of pink

think pink

This book is not just about pink – it's about the way colour can infuse the mind to create moods or feelings. It's about the power of colour to transform our environment, wherever we live. I am fascinated by the emotional impact of colour, in art, architecture and the customs of other cultures, as well as in interior decoration. Why do berry reds make us feel sexy and intense, and pale blues and lavenders calm? How can a single splash of orange alter the entire mood of a room? Why do some places lift the spirits, while others evoke a tranquil, contemplative mood? If we can only understand colour better, we can create rooms that not only look right, but feel right. This book is an attempt to explore the effects of colour on mood in a variety of very different spaces.

An original and contemporary use of colour can help you break out of conventions to create modern spaces that feel truly your own. The existing architecture may suggest a mood – but you don't have to feel tied to that initial impression. Vast modern lofts, for instance, can tempt their owners into minimalist white-on-white schemes, but is it any wonder they then feel so cold? What they often need is an injection of warm contemporary colour to bring them to life. Historic spaces hold similar pitfalls: faced with panelled walls or mullioned windows, even the most modern-minded souls retreat into the past, reaching for the heritage paint charts. But it doesn't have to be this way.

There are no rules when using colour. Feel your way into a space: imagine how you want to live in it – the parties you want to give, the paintings that inspire you. Work with moods, memories and the quality of light. You can still respect the integrity of an old manor house while painting its walls sea green. It's fine to fill a French chateau with modern furniture or hang bright sari silks at the windows. If it feels right, do it; the spaces will feel happier for it and so will you.

6

and citrus

aqua

sea green

leaf

berry

persimmon

cerise

white

pumice

lavender

blue

turquoise

The best way to begin experimenting with colour and mood is in seemingly small ways. Start by painting one wall a colour that you feel contains the essence of the mood you desire and see how the atmosphere changes. Slowly add other toning or contrasting elements until the balance feels right. That is what I have done in my London house, featured in the following pages. It constantly amazes me how just a few subtle colour changes can create an entirely different mood.

In this book, I've tried to show that modern colour can be celebrated not just in the decoration of rooms but in the details of the way we choose to live in these spaces. You can take the colour scheme of a room through to the way you arrange flowers, serve drinks or lay a table for lunch. Be spontaneous: scatter petals across a tablecloth and arrange glasses, plates and napkins in abstract patterns. Turn convention on its head in the artistry of the moment.

Make changing the moods and colours of your home a part of your way of life. Respond to the seasons by adding rugs and warmer curtains and cushions in winter, or stripping the place down for a fresher, sparser look in summer. If you feel a room needs more life, add an orange velvet cushion and a bunch of bright dahlias. If it's peace and quiet you crave, replace that huge colourful canvas with a smaller one in muted tones and remove strong contrasts and competing patterns. Move the furniture around your house and garden – the spirit of experiment keeps alive the atmosphere in a house.

One of the joys of developing your sensitivity to colour is that every day offers an opportunity to savour the satisfaction of what colour can do: a shaft of sunlight illuminating the petals of a rose; the dusty sheen of black grapes on a blue ceramic plate. And life is always the richer for such moments.

tricia guild

joyful

vivacious

serene

tranquil

contemplative

soulful

dynamic

sexy

relaxed

bright

fresh

stimulating

joyful

vivacious

mandarin

citrus

cerise

a joyful mix of colour and pattern

Often, it is the quality of natural light that leads the way when decorating a room. When this French farmhouse was modernised, huge metal-frame windows were inserted to let in the light, and the glorious sunshine that floods the room is one of the keys to its exuberant mood. Filtered first by the leaves outside and then by the bold colours and patterns on the curtains, it paints the entire room in pools of dappled sunshine. The colours were chosen to accentuate this joyful feeling. Fresh citrus shades seem to soak up the light so they can radiate sunshine even on dull days, while the bright lime greens and yellows bring the wild leafiness of the garden into the orchestrated architecture of the house. The use of translucent voiles and fine cottons at the windows ensures that none of the luminous light is lost. The colour contrasts are dynamic and unexpected – the tangy freshness of persimmon contrasting with powder pink, acid green, and touches of turquoise and yellow in the bold floral prints.

Clean lines and contrasting colour have transformed this old house into a fresh, joyful, contemporary space. There is still just a hint of the rustic in the old panelled doors and wooden beams, but the mood is upbeat and modern. The bold geometry of the modern windows contributes immeasurably to the rest of the room.

It's the dynamic mix of colour and pattern that gives the room its modern edge; the grid of the square window panes is echoed in the lines of the chairs and tables, the circles on the curtains and the spots and stripes on the cushions. The floral print on the chairs acknowledges the rural location, but forget about chintz, these are boxy clean-cut designs and the flowers are splashy, bold and modern. Mixed with bold graphic circles and brightly contrasting stripes, they challenge traditional perceptions of country style. Likewise, the real flowers in this room have a startling modern edge. Instead of big, blowsy bunches there are simple, almost minimalist combinations of flowers and foliage in plain glass vases that lift the mood and complement the clean modern shapes of the furniture. Together with the cutting edge coffee table, chairs and stools, they continue the interesting dynamic between ancient and contemporary, country and modern, that makes this room so striking.

"This dynamic mixture of colour and pattern – big graphic circles with clashing stripes and splashy modern flower prints – creates a mood of joyful spontaneity that belies the care with which the scheme was put together. The potentially wayward mixture works because of the subtle backdrop of neutrals and whites – the clean oak boards, the neutral-striped rug, the background colour of the curtains, the pair of white armchairs and other white furniture." TG

the essence of summer

Continue the mood of joyful exuberance in the way you serve food in a room. Here, a simple summer breakfast of coffee, crusty bread and jam is brought alive by the addition of fresh flower heads from the garden and sprigs of mint adorning freshly squeezed orange juice and fruit jams. The concept of breakfast in bed is comfortingly traditional, but here the presentation is unquestionably modern, with flower heads floated in water and the selection of different jams spooned into clear glass pots. A pretty white tablecloth and napkins embroidered with flowers pulls it all together and allows the bright colours to sing in the sunshine.

"When using flowers to decorate food choose their colours to complement each other and it will look as mouthwatering as it tastes. People can be reticent about using just the heads of long-stemmed flowers, but there are times when that is how they look most beautiful. And you don't necessarily need vases – these dahlias are stunning just floating on water in a simple ceramic bowl. Sprigs of fresh mint add a welcome note of green and impart their refreshing smell and flavour, making it a feast for all the senses." TG

illy

glamorous colour, sensual texture

The key to this room is the daring combination of colour and texture. Velvet is a traditional fabric, but here – thanks to the bright, vivacious colours and the clean graphic shapes

of the furniture – it looks uncompromisingly modern. The hibiscus orange, shocking pink and clear turquoise blue can all be found in the colours of the curtains – a contemporary

paisley design. What makes them work so well together is that all three have an equal intensity – no one is stronger than another, enabling them to contrast rather than conflict.

The shiny white curves of the moulded chairs, lamp and ceramics add a further exciting note of contrasting texture against the warm, worn terracotta floor.

This wonderful, high-ceilinged apartment is in a converted schoolhouse – a clean, modern, urban space with great proportions. The size of the rooms perfectly complements the tall arched windows and there is a welcome feeling of space and light above the hubbub of the city.

It can be hard to know how to arrange your life in such a large open-plan layout. Keep things simple – too many elements look cluttered and fussy while large clean shapes and clear colours build the structure you need. Here, even the textures have been confined to just two – hard and soft. All the soft furnishings are in linen – a soft yet flat texture which does not detract from the essentially square and masculine lines of the furniture. The only other textures are the hard glass, metal and shiny white surfaces of the modern tables, lamps and sideboard.

The use of colour is what creates the mood, manipulating the space, creating different atmospheres in different areas for different uses, but drawing them subtly together. Instead of keeping the place all white – the classic response to a large open-plan loft – a restricted palette of just a few strong tonal shades gives these two large adjoining rooms a sparkling vitality often lacking in such spaces.

In the upper room (right and overleaf), the orange on the sofa is a subtle shade of cantaloupe – one tone down from the zingy citrus notes seen earlier. This sits beautifully beside the fresh chartreuse of the armchair, pale ocean on the footstool, and clear crocus mauve at the windows. Just one mauve cushion on the sofa makes the crucial link with the crocus fabric at the windows.

The space flows down past the staircase into another sitting room on a lower level, with slightly smaller proportions. Here, slightly cooler colours take the mood down a note or two. But while the temperature may be cooler, the vital, vivacious mood is sustained. The ocean colours link both spaces, but the cantaloupe orange of the sofa has been exchanged for lime, with accents of turquoise in small details such as the cushions on the sofa and floor. Touches such as this help to give each room an identity of its own, even if some of the principal colours have been carried over to both.

vital, uplifting colour against a white backdrop

These are vital rather than vivid colours, with a clarity and purity that instantly lifts the spirits. A deliberately low-key backdrop of white walls and polished resin floor lets the colours sing out in the open, uncluttered space, while other details such as cushions, lamps, tables and other furniture are also confined to white.

Traditional curtains can look out of place in minimalist modern spaces, so here, banners of plain fabric have been suspended on metal rods to make simple blinds that can be opened or shut, depending on the quality of light and privacy required. They also take the colour in the room right up to the ceiling. The same window treatment has been used throughout the apartment, but in the lower room just one window panel is coloured; the rest remain pure white, which makes for a cooler feeling around the windows. White is also the predominant colour in the backdrop of walls and floor, with fresh linen cushions and a leather chair and stool.

tricia guild

a crisp striped cloth and a scattering of petals for a spontaneous al fresco lunch

shaded olive trees, summer lunch

This table laid for lunch outside has a casual, carefree charm – a mismatch of chairs brought out into the garden in the shade of old olive and fig trees. What makes it so inviting, however, is the clever use of colour that belies the seemingly spontaneous arrangement. The orange of the Arne Jacobsen chairs is highlighted on the vibrant striped tablecloth, and echoed in the flower heads strewn around the place settings and tucked into tiny vases with a few scented geranium leaves.

"Eating outside is liberating – the simple act of laying a table out of doors frees us from the formalities that might prevail in the house. Take a few risks – mix old and new, rustic and contemporary – but keep it all moving with a subtle continuity of colour. There is great fun to be had in choosing which furniture and cloths to use. Pick a favourite piece of fabric and work around it, or take some chairs that work well together and continue the scheme around those colours. Fresh salad leaves, herbs and nasturtiums from the garden make a colourful and delicious salad." TG

a feast for all the senses

Use flowers and leaves creatively to add to the spontaneous spirit of an al fresco lunch. Don't reach automatically for a jug or vase – gather flower heads from the garden or from arrangements inside the house. When the flowers in a vase begin to fade, there are always a few blooms whose beauty remains intact. Pick off those flower heads that still have life in them and scatter them over a tablecloth or display singly in little glass vases where they can be admired at close quarters. This is a great way to make the most of your flowers, even if they only last like this for a short time. They can even be kept in the fridge for a few days beforehand, if required. The heads of nerine lilies or single gladioli blooms, usually seen at the top of long stately stems and in the company of other flowers, are transformed when used in this simple, unassuming way. They add to that sense of 'contemplated haphazardness' which is so appealing but can be quite hard to achieve. Edible flowers such as nasturtiums, borage and pansies and freshly picked herbs such as chervil, coriander and basil can also be used to decorate and add taste to salads. And when serving cool drinks, such as fresh lemon pressé, fill the glass with slices of lemon or lime and use sprigs of mint to flavour the water slightly and make it more refreshing.

dancing rhythms and vibrant stripes

"The striped fabric is what draws this whole scheme together. It's perfect for this room, as it relates to the severe geometry of the floor and at the same time contains almost all the other colours that are used elsewhere. Using a plain fabric for the seats of the sofa defines its shape and gives a neutral base for the other patterns." TG

Sometimes, it is worth being as bold as you dare to breathe new life into a space. This traditional room, with its old wood panelled doors and black-and-white tiled floor, could easily look heavy and old-fashioned. Instead, it has been taken to the opposite extreme with a quirky modern mix of bright colour and graphic pattern. A real sense of joy has been brought into the space, with vivid stripes, exuberant florals and cheerful clashes bright orange, mauve, pink and canary yellow.

But there is method in the madness; the scheme is held together by a few subtle colour continuities which save it from fragmenting. The geometric floor is one anchoring force; the charcoal colour is repeated in the striped fabric on the sofas and in the floral fabrics and rug, with their scribbly, graphic, almost Fifties feel. The use of bright yellow, leapfrogging from the curtains to the floral cushions on the sofa and ottoman, is another. This is a bold look, which works because of the severity of the floor and the subtly repeating relationships between the colours – like recurring jazz themes. The flowers – tall stems of alliums or nerines, or papery rounds of ranunculus layered in stripes of colour under water – continue the quirky, graphic style.

shades of pink and persimmon with lots of white create a fresh and feminine feel

accents of orange and cerise pink

When accents of pink and orange are used in a mainly white room, the mood is warm, fresh and joyful. The grand architecture of this French chateau, with its ornate panelling, soaring ceilings and high shuttered windows, has been given a young, contemporary feel with low furniture and vivacious, feminine colour. Comfortable modern sofas and chairs are joined by lots of floor cushions; sitting on the floor in a room like this immediately makes it feel informal and relaxed. The windows are dressed in layers and stripes of various shades of pink, with gauzy voiles filtering the light like coloured glass. The pattern is a modern take on printed lace – just right for this charming flirtatious mood.

"The use of colour here is gloriously tonal – taking pink from palest shell to shocking Schiaparelli, with accents of persimmon and mauve. Colour contrast is provided by the vast expanses of white panelled walls and the oversized white rug that lightens the effect of the wooden floor. Modern combinations of hot pink dahlias, spiky grasses and scented geranium leaves give a freshness and vitality to the room." TG

pure

serene

mauve

sea green

aqua

Sometimes just one major alteration – such as repainting a wall or reupholstering a sofa – can lead the way for a number of smaller more subtle changes which combine to change the overall feeling of a room.

This large double sitting room now has a serene and tranquil air, thanks to a subtle change of colour. Walls that were once a deep turquoise have been replastered in pale *eau de nil*, which is complemented by the existing clear aqua paintwork. Bare floorboards allow the eye to run unimpeded from one end of the room to another, while translucent curtains contribute to the almost ethereal mood. The room not only looks but feels different.

Lots of pure white further lifts the space – a comfortable large sofa and modern chair are upholstered in crisp white linen, while the contemporary shapes of a white leather chair, a large Capellini floor lamp and low tables in moulded plastic and metal provide some contrasting textures. There is an interesting play between hard and soft, shiny and matt, plain and pattern, which keeps the room alive.

In such a calm and soothing space, the few splashes of contrasting colour and pattern stand out to great effect – the bold floral fabric on the floor cushion and back of a chair has as much impact as the painting on the mantelpiece. Colour and pattern have also been used to draw the two ends of the room together and make them work as one space – this can be surprisingly difficult to achieve in double sitting rooms or 'knock-through' rooms. Keeping the main upholstery colours of white and mauve the same at either end, and sprinkling accents of aqua, ocean and green in the form of cushions and other details throughout is an extremely effective way of unifying the space. Note the way the two strongest patterns – the jazzy stripe and the cut-velvet peony print – have been repeated just once in both spaces; you don't need to overdo it. The stripe on the cushions is so bold that the eye is drawn to it even at the far end of the room. The beautiful mauve and white orchid blooms are a decorative force in their own right, anchoring the eye in the centre of the room, and playing on the other mauve accents.

"This is the third change this sitting room has undergone since we've lived in this house. I wanted a softer mood while still wishing to experiment with colour – the paler walls and a lot more white have created an entirely new mood. This is a light, airy look for summer, but in winter I might use slightly more colour by laying down rugs and changing the cushions. It interests me to see how these small but subtle changes can mould the whole feeling and emotional charge of a room." TG

subtle harmonies in soft aqua and mauve make for a new calm mood

Furnishings have been kept deliberately simple in this light, uncluttered space. The absence of a rug on the floor not only makes the room feel larger, it also plays off the contrasting modern shapes and textures against a neutral, organic backdrop of pale oak boards. The mood is clear and linked by a subtle continuity of colour between the two ends of the room and by soft recurring shapes and textures. The resulting subtle harmonies are as seductive to the eye as soft music to the ear.

forget the traditions of old-fashioned flower arranging, be experimental and bold

modern flowers for a summer party

The same room has been transformed for a party with stunning modern flowers – new ways of displaying old favourites that break all the rules. A posy of sweet peas, roses and peonies is combined with towering arum lilies and a single pink nerine in a curved vase, while peonies and hydrangea heads are submerged in water, their saturated colours glowing through the glass. And there are startling uses of more flowers such as *Allium schubertii*, its glorious mauve sprays exploding from green glass like a great flowery firework. Unexpected colours, shapes and textures delight the eye at every turn – the delicacy of tiny roses and sweet peas offset by spear-like leaves and spindly seed heads.

a new mood of calm

This dining room was formerly much more rustic in style and had a completely different atmosphere – a few simple changes have changed the mood entirely. Although the colour of the wall remains the same textured lime green, this time a tiny modern painting now hangs on the wall, looking wonderfully out of scale on its huge expanse, and much more modern furniture has been used. Minimal glass-fronted metal cabinets house ceramics and glasses, while a large square table in soft grey powder-coated metal is an imposing presence in this low open space.

This room is on the lower ground floor, and has lower ceilings than the rest of the house. It could easily have ended up feeling rather dark, but the wide expanse of windows opening onto the garden, the pale stone floor and simple low shapes of the furniture keep it light and uncluttered. Against the pared-down minimalism of the table and cupboards and almost-bare wall, the snaky S-shapes of Tom Dixon's raffia chairs have a gloriously organic, almost sculptural impact and provide an interesting change of texture. In one corner of the room, where a sofa and chairs are grouped around a cosy open fire, checked fabrics and textured embroidery have been replaced by simple white linen upholstery and cushions in clear tonal shades.

a contemporary composition

However pleasing a calming, low-key space can be, you may wish to make it more lively and celebratory for a party. Be simple at the same time as being creative and add

elegance and a sense of occasion to the room without destroying its peaceful mood. Compose the table as an artist might an abstract painting – your paints are the cloths,

napkins, glasses and ceramics and, of course, the food itself.

"Create a table setting that is stimulating and adds to the air of enjoyment and anticipation. Here, four chilled soups have been elegantly arranged in lines on strips of pale linen – each with a different fresh herb leaf. The wonderful rich colours of the soups are reflected in the poppy flowers. Allow the shapes and colours of the food to set the style." TG

"Flowers can sometimes be used as sculpture. This arrangement, a variety of individual flowers in plain test-tube style glasses along a shelf, allows the beauty of the pink and white blooms to stand out against the lime green backdrop. Consider the flowers themselves and think how they might look best – this is an entirely new way of seeing a rose bud, for instance." TG

a scattering of pink rose petals for a summer celebration

softens the geometry of a London garden

midsummer garden party

This garden has a strong graphic design, with its white stone steps, clipped topiary cubes and inner sanctum within a square of pleached lime trees. With the addition of simple cube stools in soft pink, fuchsia and white, some grouped on a zinc square in the centre, the view from an upstairs window resembles an abstract painting. For the party, hundreds of pink and red rose petals have been heaped on tables and scattered on the surface of the pond – a simple yet romantic and somehow exotic touch – pervading the air with their heady scent. Soft cushions for relaxing on the terrace are shaded by simple panels of pink-and-white fabric.

tricia guild

cool, calm and contemporary

Contemporary furniture need not be confined to large modern lofts, and period features don't have to cramp your style. Mixing old and new in an interior is not only fashionable and exciting, it's a great way to breathe life into an older house, accentuating its timeless beauty in a bold and unexpected way.

This old English manor house has strong traditional architecture that could easily have dictated a dark and old-fashioned style of decorating. Instead, well-judged use of cool, clear colour and contemporary furniture has carved out a modern and soothing space, perfectly in tune with the soft east morning light that streams through the mullioned windows. The original wood-panelled walls have been washed with a beautiful soft sea-green paint, which immediately makes the space feel light and modern without clashing with its traditional features and flagstone floor. Much of the floor has been covered with a rug in palest duck-egg blue so that the modern furniture sits on a clean contemporary 'island', with just a strip of the beautifully textured old floor visible as a contrast around the edges.

The cool colours determined the choice of furniture – tables and chairs that are comfortable but uncompromisingly modern in shape, shade and texture. The black leather armchair, a modern classic with a masculine, tailored feel, is quite unexpected – the softness of the leather contrasting with the shiny metal legs. Yet it looks absolutely right, and inhabits the room almost like a piece of sculpture. The other pieces of furniture – a wonderfully comfortable club chair in ink-green bouclé wool and a large low sofa in pale ocean linen, retreat happily into the background.

There is a lot of white – on the ceiling, in the floor lamp, on the coffee table and in the voluminous linen curtains. The tall white arum lilies and alliums, fanning out into the space, perfectly suit the simple restrained elegance of this room – even the green of their stems and calyxes picks up on some of the other colours. To bring in accents of brighter colour, the curtains are edged with a bright sea-green silk cuff, and there are cushions in lime and chartreuse. These help give the room its sense of perfect balance – without them it might have felt almost too cool.

"The unexpectedness of this curvaceous, dramatic chair in the cool, calm restraint of its surroundings gives this room necessary tension. The black tailored leather brings a masculine, almost dangerous edge to the space. It doesn't appear overbearing, because subtle touches of black and charcoal in the etchings and other details help to anchor it in the room." TG

pure style and simple pleasures

elegance in the details

The old and new theme has been carried through to the details of how food and drink are served, both inside and in the garden which leads off this room. Ice cream, home-made biscuits and liqueurs are presented in a style as pure and elegant as the room itself. Mismatching antique glasses are partnered with handmade modern plates in a clear blue that picks up the darker, mauve-blue of the hydrangea heads. The touches of green in the leaves used in the flower arrangements and presentation of the food add a further 'lift' to the overall scheme of the room, bringing some of the freshness of the garden inside and the style of the interior to the garden.

"Hydrangeas are traditional garden flowers that have fallen out of fashion – but if you really look at them they are so beautiful, and their colours so subtle. Cutting off the big blowsy flower heads and arranging them in simple glass vases or under water helps one to appreciate them in a new light. It interests me to use leaves and flowers in unusual ways – these leaves, for instance, add a simple graphic touch to the plate of biscuits." TG

a peaceful mood

Soft pale green is an ideal colour for a bedroom – cool and calming but by no means cold. Here, the walls are a slightly chalky green, and there are accents of ocean, lime and *eau de nil*. This room has quite a dark wooden floor, but placing the bed on its own natural-coloured rug helps to lighten up the room, as do the translucent curtains in broad stripes of subtly different patterns. Pure crisp white linen is so welcoming on a bed, and the rather formal flower pattern on the throw – blue hydrangeas with hand-painted leaves – is a reminder that, for all its fresh modern furnishings, this is an old country house.

soulful

contemplative

shell

pumice

pebble

a space to dream

The restful feeling in this room is a result of its combination of natural colours and textures: the stone and old beams of the architecture, the warm wooden floor, the cool metal frames of the furniture, the crisp linen on the beds. Just one colour – a pale pink so soft it is almost a neutral – has been added to inject a degree of freshness and warmth. But this is not frilly, feminine pink. The clean lines of the contemporary bed and daybed are dressed and upholstered with a minimum of fuss – lots of plain linen, simple square cushions and a few panels of subtly patterned or embroidered fabric. This is a perfect space for sleeping, reading or relaxing.

Much of the room's interest lies in the surprise of finding modern furniture alongside such old architecture. The pieces have a clean-lined elegance and an unexpected lightness – the daybed on its metal frame seems almost to float above the floor, while the bed is a spare four-poster in pale brushed steel, draped with a single white muslin panel. Against the backdrop of the mullioned windows, the modern oval table and white leather chairs set up an interesting contrast in period and style.

It is easier to create a soulful mood in high-ceilinged rooms; here, to draw the eye upwards, the curtain pole has been fitted as close to the ceiling as possible and hung with banners of fabric that stretch right down to the floor. This increases the feeling of height in the room and makes the windows appear larger. White muslin with a fine pink stripe filters the sun and floods the room with soft hazy light – the panel of fabric can be pulled into different positions along the rail as required. The slim uprights of the modern four-poster emphasise the strong vertical element, as does the tall slice of mirror propped up against the wall. The minimalist arrangements of white alliums, pink nerines and single orchid and gladioli blooms are the perfect complement to the still and tranquil mood. Beautiful and graceful without being fussy, the bright pink of the blooms highlights the subtler use of pink elsewhere.

The details in a neutral room make all the difference, and they can easily be changed to create a new mood. Here, the only accessories are tonal – in deeper or richer shades of pink or subtle stripes and patterns.

"Light, feminine fabrics on the bed and at the window bring a dreamy quality to this otherwise quite cool contemporary bedroom, and form a bridge between the old beams and mullions and the modern furniture. Just a single piece of crushed fine linen muslin softens the clean metal frame of the four-poster, making it romantic but still resolutely modern. The curtain is a banner of the same muslin that will float anywhere along the rail." TG shell pink so pale and soft it's barely there

a sunlit breakfast table for a gentle start to the day

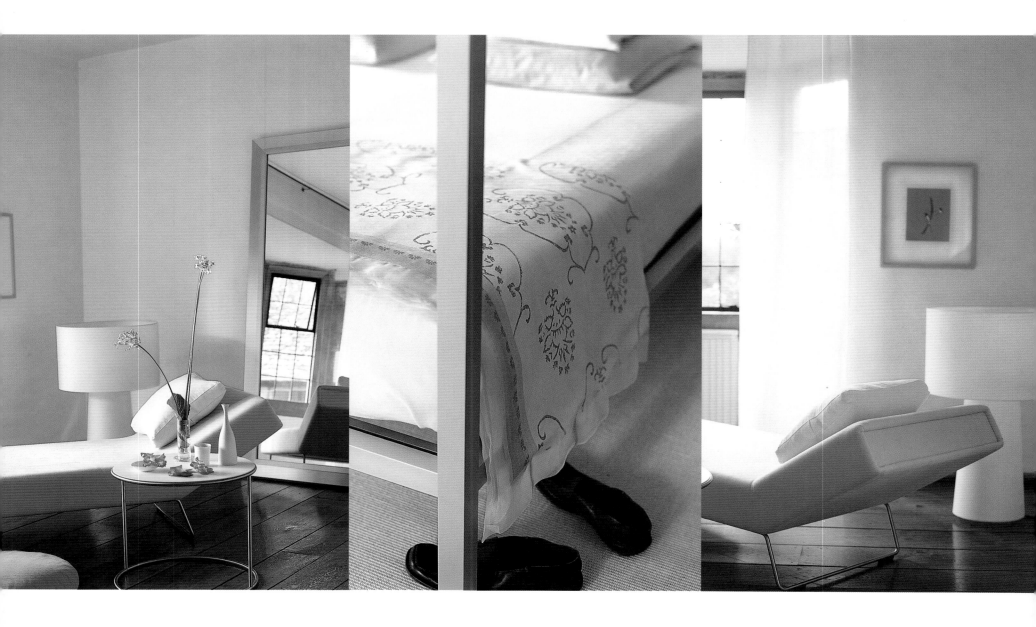

It takes courage to use such modern furniture in an old house, but it works if you are consistent. Everything here is very clean-cut and graphic, from the modern four-poster to the light metal frames of the day bed and tables. There is a balance of square, geometric and curvaceous rounded shapes – they play off one another in a satisfying way. The soft, dreamy touches are in the details – in the scattering of pink gladioli blooms on the table and the delicately patterned bedspread. There is so little pattern elsewhere in this room that one notices even the tiniest details, like the hand-painted scrolling designs on the fabric.

"Old and new contrast
harmoniously in the
circular white table and
white leather chairs by
the old mullioned windows.
There's even a quiet
thoughtfulness in the way
the table has been laid for
breakfast. It might take
a little extra effort to
bring everything up to the
bedroom and arrange the
fruit compote and yoghurt
in little glasses with sprigs
of mint, but the reward
is a beautiful, clear start
to the day." TG

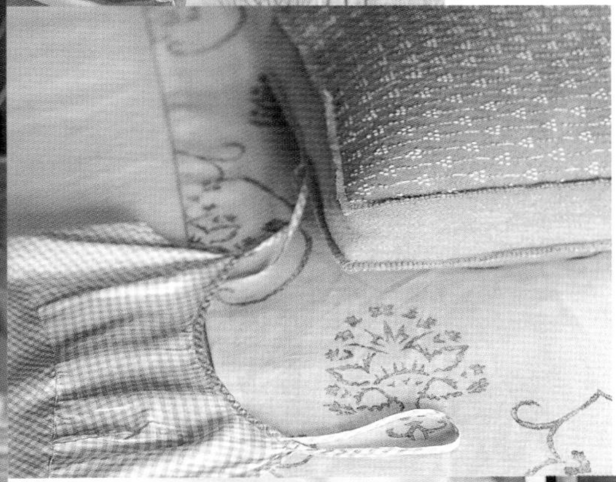

There is a masculine but nonetheless tranquil atmosphere in this tiny apartment in an old Italian palazzo. With an abundance of distinctive architectural features, the aim was to make the studio flat feel clean, uncluttered and modern. Paring down the colour and keeping the furniture simple was the key to success, and the tiled floor was painted grey throughout to unify the space. The modern steel kitchen is a miniature model of efficiency, while brushed aluminium tables and cabinets look light and elegant in a soft grey. This is a far cry from soulless minimalism, however – touches such as a propeller-style ceiling fan and the metal floor lamps give the place an air of individuality and character. It is the perfect male pied-à-terre – a peaceful haven when one wants solitude, but with the potential to become a practical, sociable base for entertaining.

Grey is the predominant colour, with matt and shiny metal sitting easily alongside the various tonal shades. An absence of stronger colours makes one more aware of the variations in shades and textures and the different moods that the various materials evoke. One principal piece of furniture – a wedge of a modern sofa in pale blue-grey linen – presides over the main space; other seating consists of informal floor cushions and woven rope chairs on light metal frames. The transparent quality of this natural weave adds a new texture and makes the space feel open and uncluttered.

In all this modernity, the magic of a real fire has not been forgotten, and a contemporary fireplace has been cut into a long low opening in the wall. The result is unquestionably modern, but still preserves the tradition of glowing embers and wood smoke, most welcome in the cold Tuscan winters. The low furniture is grouped informally around a rug with a geometric design in the same tonal colours, creating a quiet yet intimate mood. The metal lamps inject a slightly humorous note, and their light unobtrusive structure is the perfect complement to the rope chairs and table.

Essentially this is an exercise in the use of non-colour, but touches of mauve raise the prevailing greys onto a richer, more soulful plane. Flowers, a matt vase and the odd cushion keep the mauve theme moving through the various different rooms – the space would feel much colder and over-masculine without them.

"The floor tiles are painted a soft grey, which has helped to lighten and unify the space. A slightly richer grey border has been painted around the base of the walls – a modern take on a traditional Italian decorating device which gives weight to the room and balances the fine tubular furniture. Grey paint has also been used for windows and doors giving shape, and a reminder that we are within an ancient building." TG

splashes of impromptu colour bring a blank canvas to life

In such a small apartment, the same mood, colours and details carried through all the rooms create a restful harmony and make the space feel larger. The tiny bedroom is just big enough for a double bed on a brushed steel frame, some modern metal storage units and a white moulded plastic chair for clothes. The contemporary kitchen carries on the theme with angular stainless steel units echoing the grey-on-grey scheme of the rest of the apartment.

"In this neutral environment even the most casual, throwaway gestures have a startling graphic impact and any other colour added to the mix, even temporarily, really sings out. Slices of orange in a drink, a spotted red tie slung across a chair or a bowl of bright lemons on a table are like splashes of bright paint on a white and grey canvas." TG

In this London apartment, different shades of greys have been used in the sitting room while oatmeal tones bring a subtly different look to the bedroom (overleaf). Both looks are contemporary and slightly masculine in feel while sacrificing nothing to comfort. One could imagine reading for hours undisturbed in this peaceful room.

The temptation with natural schemes is to create textural contrasts, but here that has been kept to a minimum, resulting in an almost palpable sense of stillness. In the sitting room, the predominant textures are quite dry: thick grey emulsion on one wall, a coarse cotton duck for the grey striped curtains and dove flannel on the sofa. The metal in the room has a soft sheen rather than a shine – the brushed aluminium of the minimalist cupboard, the gleam of a lamp, the finish on the salvaged and stripped-down radiator. Even the floor – old boards painted white and worn down with wear – has a flatness that is appropriate. Flowers and other objects are kept to a minimum – white eucharists in clear glass vases and a few specially chosen ceramics.

Greys work well together. For deeper accents, go for charcoals, rather than the browner shades and taupes that might sit uneasily in the scheme. Mixing grey neutrals with browns and creams is often extremely tricky. In this scheme, the oatmeal shades have been confined to the bedroom (overleaf), thus creating a completely different look while remaining within the overall neutral palette.

One wall in the bedroom has been covered in a subtle flower print – a Japanese-style design that is echoed on the bed linen. Pattern is unexpected in a minimal scheme – particularly one with such a masculine feel – but this design is about as pared down as floral gets and contributes to the mood of calm. Again, textures are surprisingly dry – the curtains here are no-nonsense flannel, an unusual choice in a bedroom but with an under-layer of light voile that plays against it and injects a note of softness. The bedcover is also flannel, in a deeper chocolate shade, but with piles of soft pillows and cushions, one in richly-patterned silk. The shapes in these rooms may be gloriously spare – the wide, low bed with its pale wood bedhead, the minimalist metal tables and lamps – but the overall feel is one of comfort.

"Neutral tones can be de-sensitising, so add some life in the form of depth of tone. Here, I've included charcoal among the cooler paler greys in the sitting room and cocoa brown amid the oatmeal shades of the bedroom. The textures are quite cool and dry, but a few softening touches make all the difference – the velvet nap of a cushion, the fragility of white flower petals, the gossamer voile of the under curtains soften the scheme without compromising its masculinity." TG

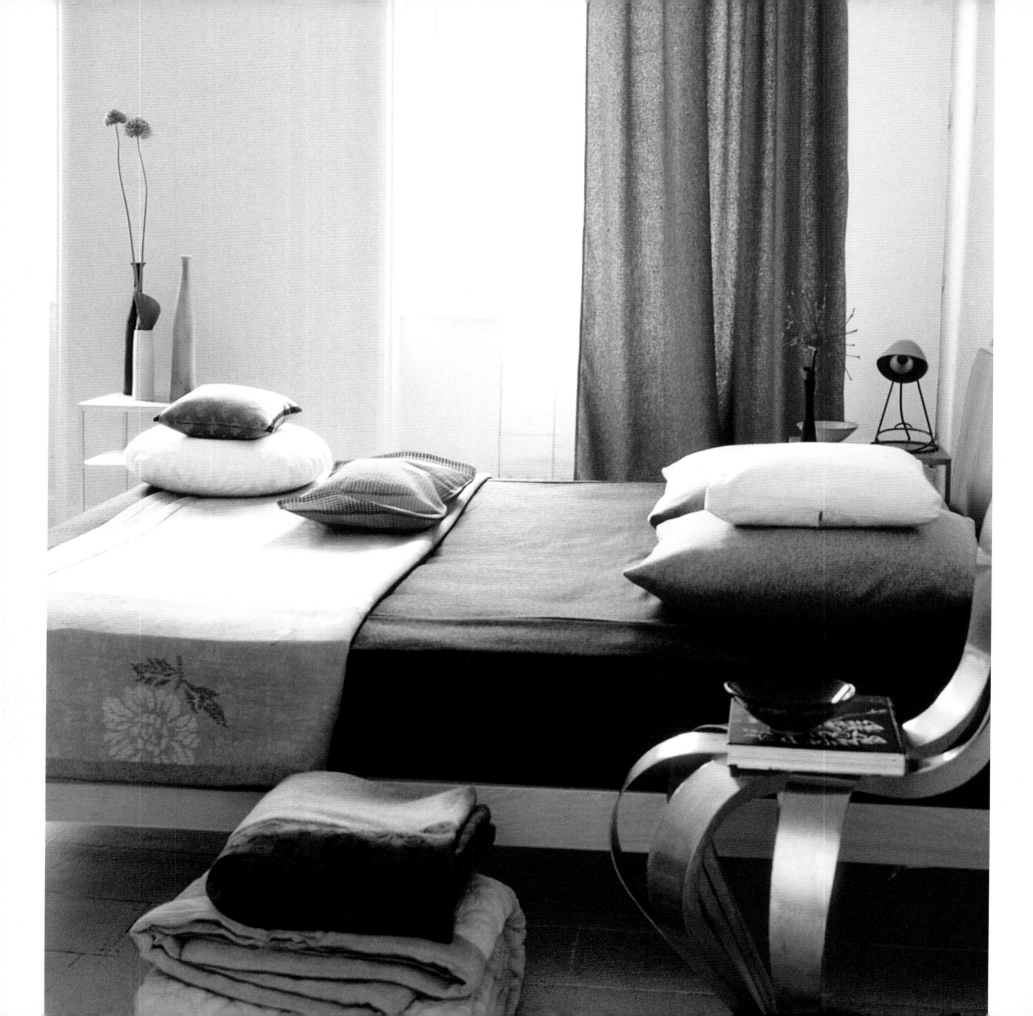

Without the subtle flower design on one wall behind the bed, this minimalist bedroom might have looked hard and soulless. A few such touches soften the room slightly but just enough: the contemporary bed has piles of pillows and cushions – most of them plain but one in delicately patterned silk; the flannel curtains have a layer of translucent voile beneath. Even the sheen of the curved metal chair beside the bed brings a subtle change of shape and texture. The chocolate-brown bedspread contributes a welcome warm, dark tone among all the creams and oatmeals – a room composed entirely of pale naturals could be rather dull.

using chalky shades of pink in a cool, contemporary way

softly sophisticated

With its concrete floors and bare plaster walls, this cool modern space called out for a restrained contemporary look, but it was important that it did not become cold and impersonal. Using pink in a totally modern way was an inspired move, and the soft blossom sofa led the way. The shape is low and simple, contemporary yet comfortable, yet upholstered in leather or dark wool it would have dictated a completely different mood. Here, like a classic, beautifully tailored suit in a clear unexpected colour, the effect of the pale pink is charming, immediately bringing a lightness of touch that is carried through to the flowers and other details.

timeless natural textures

What more peaceful combination of colours to sleep surrounded by than shades of off-white and cream? Natural colours and textures come into their own in bedrooms, where you are aiming for a still contemplative atmosphere without too many distractions. They are also a good way of pulling together a mix of different periods and styles, surfaces and textures. If your palette is restricted to a few shades, the colours and textures of different materials can be seen at their best: wood with its variety of tones and grains, rough or polished stone, shiny or matt metal, starched or soft-washed linen. Rather than fight against one another or get lost in a cacophony of clashing colours, each material has room to breathe and to work together with the others to create an integral whole.

The natural harmony of this beautiful bedroom relies on a wide range of natural materials. The ancient, slightly rough texture of the stone at the windows and the warm brown floorboards are part of the original architecture of the house. To this has been added the even richer dark brown of an antique chest of drawers, the gloriously organic shape and texture of Tom Dixon's raffia 'S' chair, some cool brushed modern metal in the form of lamps and tables, crisp white upholstery and bed linen and the pale blonde wood of the contemporary bed itself. Too large an expanse of dark wooden floor can make even the sunniest room look gloomy; here, this is avoided with a pale rug that brings the illusion of more light into the room.

When you are using neutrals, it's easy to get so caught up in the subtleties of tones and textures that you forget about pattern. But even in completely neutral tones, a beautiful print or pattern can add a glamorous softness to a room, while in no way disturbing the disciplined colour palette. The curtains in this bedroom have a beautiful, hydrangea pattern in white, dove grey and silver. Bed linen and upholstery are confined to the palest shades, with just the subtlest gold, silver and grey printed detail on the bedcover.

"Different woods don't always sit happily together. The pale new ash of this modern bed didn't seem right on the warm old floorboards until we added a plain neutral rug to ease the transition. The different tones and types of wood work as colours and textures in their own right, but they need to be balanced with other elements in the room." TG

The juxtaposition of styles makes one look at both in a new light. In this bedroom, the play of antique against modern creates an interesting dynamic: period architecture, wooden floorboards, a contemporary bed and chair and a superb antique walnut chest of drawers in the corner. The surprise of this old piece alongside all the more modern furniture really highlights the beauty of its warm colour and patina. The contemporary ceramics and stylised flower arrangements placed on it maintain the playful tension right down to the details. And the curtain fabric – an almost formal flower print with a fresh modern twist – pulls old and new together, creating a well-balanced and cohesive whole.

dynamic

sexy

persimmon

berry

rose

André Breton

People are often frightened to use hot pinks and reds in a modern, minimalist space, but warm colours can bring a real sense of dynamism. The sitting room in this modern house in France is just such a cool, clean-cut space, but curvaceous furniture and rich voluptuous colours make it sexy and dynamic rather than cold and clinical. The use of colours, shapes and textures that are warm and sensual but not over-feminine prevents the scheme from becoming too decorative. There are no patterns here, and the rich colours are countered by lots of white and neutrals. Though the overall impression is one of colour, the vibrant shades are used only for the furnishings and textiles rather than on the walls, which are left white, or the floor, which is unadorned. This preserves the sense of perfect balance in the space. The mood could be changed again by adding a wall of dynamic colour to the space.

The deepest colour is concentrated in the cyclamen mauve of the large three-seater sofa that defines the main seating area, and in the full billowing curtains, in a lighter crocus shade with a thick border the same shade as the sofa. The chair is pale clematis, with cushions of white linen, clematis silk and a wonderful persimmon which seems to energise all the subtler pinks and mauves. Imagine the effect of taking that one persimmon cushion away – the whole mood would drop a notch.

Not only are the colours voluptuous and sensual, the shapes are soft and curvy too. Modern furniture is often thought of as linear and hard-edged, but the generous flowing shapes of the contemporary sofa, white plastic chair and clematis armchair illustrate the comfortable side of modernism. The soft shapes of the furniture mean that some of the details can be more architectural – the square metal table and boxy lamp, for instance, are quite hard-edged.

Textures have been chosen to warm up the scheme still further. The sofa is upholstered in the softest cashmere wool – also used at the windows to warm up the minimal floor-to-ceiling panes. Crisp white linen or leather might have been an obvious choice for the upholstery, but the mood would have become too cool. The chair is covered in looped bouclé wool, which is comfortable but still very contemporary.

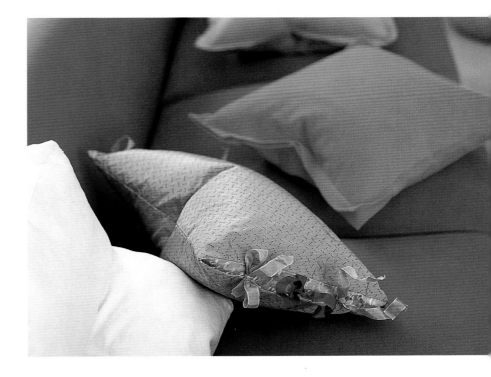

"In one sense, the scale is all wrong with these tall spindly foxgloves on a low table in a lofty white room. But they work – it is not just the colour or their wayward curves, but also the sense that they are wild woodland flowers in this very contemporary setting. They bring a note of eccentricity that I love. It's also there in the one persimmon cushion – it's somehow amusing, eccentric, sexy. It says that you're not playing safe." TG

"This large, high-ceilinged room in a French chateau could easily have looked too traditional, but an unusual and dramatic choice of colours – lime green and turquoise contrasted with raspberry pink and crimson – brings it right into the twenty-first century. This patterned flower fabric used for the curtains was inspired by ancient costumes from Uzbekistan – another example of classical origin contemporary design." TG

brilliant modern colour in an old French chateau

dazzling intensity

Lime green and turquoise are seldom used in this way with raspberry pink and crimson, but here the clean contrast is fresh and inviting, the greens and blues cooling down the heat of the rich berry shades. The beautiful bold flower print of the curtains takes the colour right up to the soaring ceilings, and acts as a bridge between the traditional architecture of this French chateau, with its imposing windows, ornate detailing and crystal chandelier, and the modern shapes and colours of the furnishings. The design of the print has a classic feel, but it has been given a modern twist and partnered with patterned borders and an inner curtain of bright turquoise muslin.

Furniture has been confined to low, contemporary shapes – a long sofa in bright lime green velvet, generously wide armchairs in pink and turquoise, and a square white table resting close to the ground. Contrary to what one might expect, long, low furniture looks great in a high room, further adding to the sense of drama. The feeling of air and space in the room encourages one to take further risks with colour, placing a crimson peony print panel on the lime sofa, and a chartreuse cushion on a pink velvet chair. The peony print has been echoed by real peonies in vases on tables – their voluptuous blowsy blooms are perfect for the grand, almost opulent feeling in this room. Again, their different intensities of pink are countered by the cool green of a curvaceous hosta leaf.

strawberry red and hot zinnia pink, slices of juicy watermelon

colours to make your heart sing

The table is laid in Tuscany for an impromptu early evening drink with friends. Slices of luscious watermelon look great on a bright batik cloth with lots of little zinnia flowers, gathered from the garden and placed in individual containers with a few leaves. It's a simple spontaneous arrangement that catches the exact mood of the hour, as if the colours of a summer sunset have been drawn down on to the table – vibrant crimsons, reds and oranges with just a hint of cooling green in the hosta, vine and mint leaves.

"All the flowers on these pages were grown and gathered in my cutting garden. We grow poppies in all shades from pale pink through scarlet and crimson to deepest purple-black, as well as zinnias, sweet peas, scented geraniums and dahlias, and I'm constantly amazed by the way the rich beauty of their shapes and colours changes with the light. One of my greatest passions is choosing flowers and trying new combinations of colours and textures, hoping to create magic." TG

jewel-bright silks and pared-down sensuality

a sense of romance

Banners of shot silk in jewel-bright pink, red and mauve are the only adornment at these elegant French windows. The rich colours glow with even more intensity with the

sunlight shining through them, and bathe the entire room in a soft sensual glow. The mood is romantic without being over-feminine – indeed the arrangement is almost minimal;

with cooler colours and no cushions an entirely different atmosphere would be created. The clean lines of the modern daybed are covered in plain lilac bouclé wool and all

the decorative detail is concentrated in the cushions – exquisite concoctions in embroidered silks, ikat weaves and painterly florals that pick up on the principal colours.

Rich reds and pinks in bold prints and ikats create a warm and sultry mood in this beautiful old French room. Ikat patterns have an exotic opulent feel that conjures up the languid luxury of Middle Eastern palaces; used here on a low modern daybed with piles of soft pillows and floor cushions all around, they bring a contemporary feeling to a traditional interior.

A room such as this, with its high ceilings and imposing architectural mouldings, seems to demand a dramatic touch. The tall windows provide a great opportunity to use large patterns and to experiment with a succession of different layers of varying weights and textures. Lined printed linen, unlined silk brocade and transparent silk muslin have been added like layers of paint on canvas to create a feeling of incredible richness. The curtains can be pulled across at different times and in different combinations to create a range of subtle and shimmering effects that change with the light and the seasons, altering the mood of the entire room.

This scheme manages to incorporate the whole spectrum of reds and pinks, from deep berry purples through scarlet and crimson to paler pinks and mauves. There is even a shot of bright persimmon in the cushions and on the broad cuff at the base of the curtains. Using all these shades together is a bold move that requires a sure hand. It works here because of the preponderance of neutrals in the existing architecture of the room. Surfaces are relatively unsophisticated, with subtly textured bare plaster walls and floors covered with hexagonal terracotta tiles. The raw pinkish materials act as a warm but neutral colour in the room and help to balance the ikat weaves and textured silks; they might otherwise have felt almost oppressively opulent. Even the ikat patterns themselves have neutral shades printed or woven in alongside the richer colours, making them easy to use alongside other, more complex designs.

In spite of the rich mood, the furniture in the room is very simple. The design of the daybed is clean and minimalist, and the little bleached wood table and the console fashioned from a slab of walnut fit perfectly into the scheme – their raw natural materials providing an earthiness that is welcome in such a grand room.

"This room is made for relaxing. The low shapes of the furniture, the ikat daybed with its piles of pillows and the luxurious silk floor cushions all contribute to the sultry laid-back mood. The dominant horizontal shapes are countered by the long silk curtains, and the wide band of pure persimmon silk at the base of the curtains is a dynamic and interesting detail that links them back to other elements in the room." TG

layer upon layer of sensual silks and brocades

soft cushions piled high on furniture and floor

Warm neutral textures on the walls and floor make it possible to be bold with colour and pattern. Mixing all tones of red and pink from scarlet through crimson to candy is

not often done, but the shades used here are within the same essential colour range, hotted up by the odd touch of persimmon or deep berry, so the result is a harmonious

combination. Feminine touches are confined to the details: the frill on a bolster, the pink silk ribbons on a cushion and the pretty posies of flowers on shelves and tables.

"I've used all shades of red and pink in this room - pushing the combinations as far as they can go whilst maintaining the sultry harmonious mood. Tradition has it that such colours clash, but they all fall within the same sort of tonal family - and anyway, what does clashing mean? The scheme works because of the warm neutrals in the raw plaster walls and tiled floors. All colour and pattern is confined to the textiles, so why not experiment with lots of different patterns and textures? A room like this can take some eccentric touches." TG

berry shades cut with citrus notes for a fresh dynamic mood

vibrant contrasts

The greyish-white plaster on the walls in this room demanded a fresher colour scheme. The hot berry shades on the sofa are cooled down by the other colours in the room to create a lighter, more romantic mood. Notes of citrus and chartreuse cut through the sensual pinks and reds, and the flower arrangements are fresh and modern. The curtains are made from an ikat weave in fresh lavender, with layers of translucent silk behind and a cuff of bright lime green. Lots of white keeps the mood light and uplifting – white tables, sculptural lamps and moulded plastic chairs – with a large round white cushion adding a note of contrast on the sofa.

"Curtains are so often used too traditionally. I don't think you always have to match curtains in pairs – using panels or banners of different colours or patterns is a more modern way to bring interest to a room. The curtains here are in a lavender ikat weave with other panels in pale translucent silks. I've also used pattern in the rug – a vibrant voluptuous image in soft lavenders and greys that cools the pinkish ochre of the floor and helps to define the space." TG

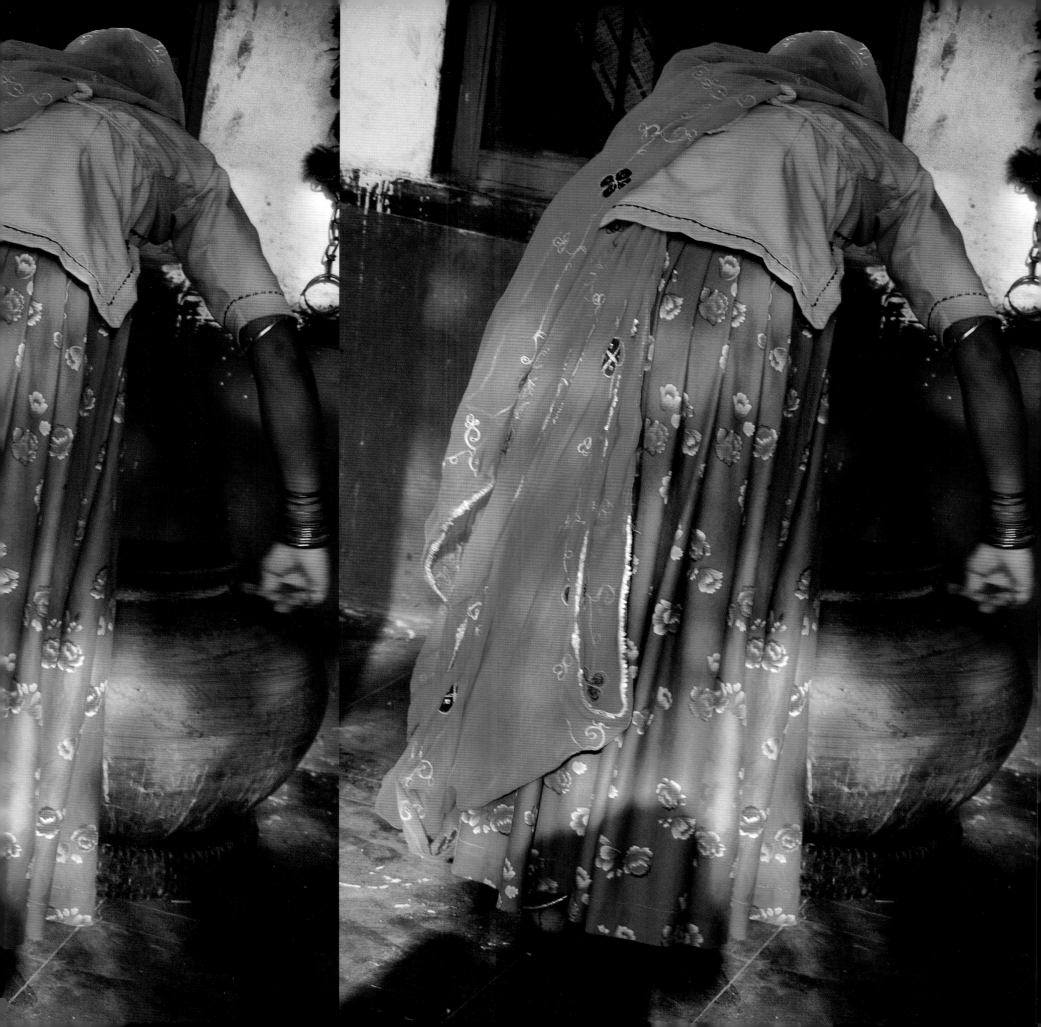

Opening your kitchen cupboard can be as exciting as dipping into a box of paints, with as much potential for creativity. Think of every meal or party as a different picture, with the table as your blank canvas. Why use the same old mats, plates, glasses and table linen for every meal? Selecting and combining different tableware for different occasions is a quick and easy way to change the entire mood of a room – and it can be great fun, too. Mix and match different styles and colours to complement the food and the mood. Either start with the food you want to serve and go with the colours and textures it suggests, or for a special occasion decide on the mood first and fit the food around it.

In many ways, serving food is as sensual and creative as decorating a room. The natural colours and textures of food are as inspiring as the finest silks and fabrics; their shapes as suggestive as sculpture. Picture the dark glossy sheen of fresh cherries, the soft gleam of fish scales, the curvaceous contours of a cantaloupe melon. Plan your menu to look as good as it tastes, and create interesting contrasts in the accompanying salads and sauces. Plates, linen and glasses can be chosen to complement the food, but keep the style simple and let your cooking do the talking.

The modern approach to table decoration is to keep colours down to one or two shades with maybe a contrasting accent colour, and use mats, cloths or linen runners to make simple abstract patterns on the table. There's no need to do anything fiddly with napkins – crisp linen loosely folded is perfect. The advantage of minimalist flower arrangements is that they take up less space on the table. Just scatter a few petals across the table or on a tray full of puddings to add an air of casual romance.

Sometimes the simple beauty of fresh fruit, for instance, is best left unadorned. But rather than just presenting it on a plate, try layering berries in different colours in a glass bowl with stripes of mint or basil leaves. Or bring a charming modern twist to a traditional recipe with an unusual container, such as the luscious panna cotta (opposite) served in painted Moroccan tea glasses.

"It's important to create a sense of occasion, exciting the senses by presenting food in simple yet beautiful ways. Eating with friends can be a real celebration for all the senses – it is so enriching to take the time to try to make a magical atmosphere using flowers, leaves and the food itself, combining all the delicious tastes and textures." TG harmonious colours and a scattering of flowers create a fun and festive atmosphere

For this summer dinner party the dining room table is given a bright new look, with round felt mats in hot berry shades and vases of pink peonies, hyacinths and nerines. Serving simple food in exotic and imaginative ways creates a light-hearted festive air. Here, fresh berries are suspended in fruit jelly so that their colours make a pattern of stripes in clear glass tumblers; clear ice buckets are lined with layers of strawberries, blueberries, cherries, and mint leaves; and panna cotta is poured into painted tea glasses. The jellies are decorated with blossoms and single petals are scattered around the food.

"The way food is served can be so visually exciting and individual – not about fussy ideas, just simple yet imaginative touches like serving panna cotta in these vibrant Moroccan glasses with rose petals bordering the plates in strips. Find inspiration in the contrasting colours and graphic shapes of the food itself, and from different glasses and ceramics." TG

relaxed

restful

lavender

blue

indigo

The quality of light coming through the slashes of glass in the roof gives this room the air of an artist's studio. One wall was formerly a strong cobalt blue, which dominated the mood and made for a dynamic lively contrast with the books and ceramics collected on the shelves. The change of colour to palest lavender on that wall and soft white plaster for the others has lowered the temperature and brought the room much more into line with its function as a study. The calmer colours make it feel much more like a working space, perfect for developing ideas or relaxing with a book. At the far end, a simple glass-topped table is used as a desk, but work in progress can be shut away in the modern metal cupboard behind. In the middle of the room, low moulded plastic chairs are grouped around the coffee table – comfortable as well as elegant, they are upholstered in clear shades of linen.

The reorganisation of the space means it works well as a private study, and can easily be put to more sociable use. The conservatory is used more in summer, when the metal doors at the far end can be thrown open and a table and chairs taken out to the terrace overlooking the garden. In winter, heaters prevent too much heat loss through the roof, while a rug might be added for extra warmth underfoot.

Along one wall, treasured ceramics and vases of flowers are arranged for their intrinsic beauty and the inspiration they provide. To further pare down the space and calm the mood, the objects have been ruthlessly edited; the tableaux of ceramics, books and flowers is now as restful and inspiring as a still life by Giorgio Morandi. The objects can be changed from time to time to alter the mood.

Reducing this room to its architectural elements and toning down the colour has made it a more neutral space – a stage set in which the colours of flowers, books and other favourite objects can create their own impromptu drama. Cutting out clutter can be tremendously liberating, and is claimed to improve concentration. The increased feeling of space also creates room for nature's own artistry – for the fleeting patterns of light and shade, sun and cloud to work their own subtle magic on the pale concrete floor and across the pale walls.

ice cream and cake served in a cool contemporary setting

For a simple summer tea in the conservatory, scoops of ice cream and wedges of chocolate cake are served in simple glass containers on a clean white background and scattered with just a few blossoms from a vase of pink hyacinths and tall white alliums.   The gracious curve of a hosta leaf makes an impromptu mat, and sprigs of mint have been added to the refreshing herb tea, served from a clear modern teapot.   Contemporary tableware and linen in a beautiful clear turquoise is a good foil for the sweeter pinks and mauves of the flowers.

"Nothing could be more traditionally English than the idea of afternoon tea, in this case with the added delicious luxury of home-made ice cream and chocolate cake. But the choice of simple clear glass containers, a cool white background and touches of the palest mauves, pinks and blues transforms the setting. This is a new way of being romantic – the feeling is there but in a modern, minimalist style." TG

There is a wonderfully serene feel to this sitting room, with its high ceilings and pale grey plaster walls, and the quality of light from the windows is almost ethereal. Sometimes a single fabric provides the starting point for an entire colour scheme; here, the large-scale blue lily print used for the curtains has a strong sophisticated feel that helps establish the mood of the room. Blue has a reputation as a cold colour, but this is a warm shade with a certain amount of red in it. It's a bold choice, and the same clear china blue has been continued on the sofa and chair, and picked up in the delphiniums and hydrangeas in the flower arrangements.

This room is all about harmony rather than contrast, so the accent colours of magenta and soft pink were taken from the colours in the centre of the blooms. These colours are picked up in the silk ribbon trim of the curtains, the pink linen chair, the patterns on the abstract rug and the simple vases of dahlias. There is also quite a lot of white, which complements the wonderful quality of the light. The restrained use of colour, with an emphasis on subtle continuity between the different elements in the room, is what keeps the mood restful and relaxed.

Colour, light and texture work harmoniously together to create an atmosphere that is both restful and interesting, seductive yet still cool. Textures range from the crisp starched linen of the curtains to a softer brushed linen on the sofa, chairs and ottoman, and luxurious velvet for the cushions. A scheme such as this can be enhanced still further, even temporarily, by adding apparently clashing elements in the form of flowers and cushions in contrasting colours. The surprise of an orange cushion on a blue chair lifts the mood and adds a touch of dynamic energy. The room doesn't rely on this, but it illustrates the impact that just a few tiny touches of unexpected colour can have.

"I've always been drawn to blues and mauves. I find these colours incredibly calming but also quite sensual. The shade of blue in this room is warm – it has quite a lot of red in it – and it has been further warmed by the other colours with which it is mixed: magenta, crocus, orange, the deep pink of a dahlia bloom." TG

tall blue flowers in an elegant setting

bold printed fabric echoed in a modern nature study

The large-scale blue-and-white fabric used for the curtains sets the tone of quiet sophistication in this stunning sitting room, the style and colours of the print echoed in the multiple display of flowers on the modern console table. The flower arrangements are romantic yet modern, bringing a sense of lightness to the room that is quite easy to achieve. Irises, delphiniums and white peonies have been arranged in the same spirit of the lily print fabric – the individual blooms displayed in a row of clear glass vases like a modern botanical study.

soft shades and charming patterns

This charming attic bedroom has been transformed through a creative combination of colour and pattern. The sloping walls were a real challenge, and the unusual choice to paper them really paid off. A delightful sprigged cornflower print which is repeated, slightly larger, at the windows, has exactly the right rustic credentials for a rural house, but is fresh and modern rather than countrified. To emphasise the height in what could easily appear to be a poky space, the curtain rail has been hung as high as possible on the wall, with the fabric dropped in a long sweeping banner to the floor.

Confining the colours to one or two neighbouring tones works well within a small room such as this. Lavender and lilac are soft and pretty but still have a fresh contemporary edge. Clever use has been made of paint here – the far wall is a fresh clear shade of mauve, which helps to unify the room, and the floorboards are a slightly lighter shade of the same colour.

The ancient wooden beams have been left unpainted, however, to provide a reminder of the room's origins and to make a visual link with the new wood of the bed and other modern furniture. The raw wood textures of the beautifully designed modern cabinet strikes just the right note between rustic and modern, as do the hydrangeas on top of it. A winged armchair is another traditional classic, but this one has quirky curly arms and is upholstered in crisp lilac linen. There is just a touch of contrasting colour in the striped pillowcase and pink floral patterns on the bedcover. Otherwise, nothing disturbs the restful and relaxing atmosphere.

Paint can be a great way to breathe new life into potentially poky spaces. The narrow twisting staircase leading up to this bedroom has been transformed with a coat of palest blue on the walls and a slightly darker shade on the stairs themselves, with fresh white for the skirting boards and door posts. When wood – even old wood – is unremarkable or in bad condition, it often makes more sense to paint it than strip and polish it. And if it gets chipped or dirty or you just fancy a change, it is easy enough to repaint it.

"Look at the wonderful contrast between the gnarled old wood of the ancient beams and the smooth polished grain of this modern cabinet. The key to this attic room is taking traditional shapes and spaces and giving them a subtle modern twist. Even these blue hydrangeas – the classic country garden flower – are modern when used with hosta leaves and a single purple calla lily." TG

"When drawn, the banner of fabric at the window of this tiny bedroom can be admired almost like a painting, making a link with the flower-printed wallpaper. The floor-length swathe of fabric also has the effect of making the window seem larger and the space more modern and sophisticated – the metal curtain rail taken as high as possible to accentuate the length." TG

relaxed comfort among the olive trees in an Italian country garden

a contemporary outdoor room

Life spills out of the house into the garden in summer, and the square gravel terrace is as restful and relaxed as an indoor sitting room, providing a transition from the interior to the wilder garden beyond.   The 'green architecture' has a graphic formality: the low box hedges act as walls to contain the space, while the clipped topiary cones and spheres are like living furniture or sculpture.   Within this formal structure, the mood is spontaneous and relaxed, with chairs and small tables gathered in casual groups beneath the trees.   Opening off to the side, in the shade of a simple pergola covered in vines, is a smaller, more enclosed space that is often used for dining.

"This farmhouse sits in a rural landscape, and the garden, with its orchard and olive trees, is quite rustic. But I felt the need for a slightly more formal area near the house – this square of gravel with its box edging gives strong definition, creating graphic tension between the landscape and living areas. The furniture is mainly light, modern and relaxed, with one or two rustic contemporary pieces." TG

classic calm blue and white

This little attic bedroom has been transformed into an airy modern space. Lots of pale blue has created a calm mood – the cherry blossom print on the walls has an oriental

feel, while pale paint on the floorboards reflects light from the window. Two single beds are simply covered in white linen, with throws and pillows that inject the only notes of

stronger colour – fresh limes and yellows with just a touch of clear pink. Clean modern furniture – a curvy metal frame chair and metal table and cupboard – creates a pleasing

contrast with the original beams and old-fashioned latch door.

"We haven't been precious about original features in this attic room. It was a wise choice to paint the old floorboards and door – only the ancient ceiling beams have been left with their rough organic texture exposed. This preserves a sense of warmth and history in the room and adds to the exciting mix of old and new." TG

restful lavender pink

The mood in this attic bedroom follows the architecture: romantic and verging on traditional but just a little quirky. The floral fabric at the window is quite formal, as is the use of patterned wallpaper, but there are just enough contemporary details to give the room a modern edge. The sleek metal bedside table, the cool grey and white ceramics, the banner of mauve and turquoise striped silk on the bed, and the idiosyncratic flower arrangements bring it right up-to-date. Flowers such as these are usually seen in great gaudy bunches – displaying them individually shows off each bloom for the miniature work of art that it is.

"This shade of lavender almost crosses over into pink – ideal for the romantic restful mood of this tiny attic bedroom. Large furniture can work in small rooms if they are kept uncluttered. Here, a big old-fashioned double bed almost fills the space, but simple shapes, light coloured fabrics and lots of white bed linen make it feel bright and welcoming. The damask wallpaper gives a soft subtle pattern and colour. A tonal scheme in shades of mauve is gentle on the eye, with just one or two subtle accents of turquoise, red and orange in the bedspread and flowers." TG

fresh

stimulating

turquoise

lime

leaf

This open-plan studio has different areas for sitting and dining. The feeling is cool, and industrial, with modern metal-frame windows along one side, white walls and a pale concrete floor, but the unexpected use of three colours – ocean blue, crocus and just a touch of tangerine – gives it real warmth. These fresh colours seem to breathe new life into the room, as do the simple silk curtains billowing in the breeze. Modern spaces often seem still and static, with their air conditioning systems and fixed closed windows, but here, a sense of spontaneity seems to fill the room along with the fresh air. The mauve and orange on the furniture are picked out in the subtle striped borders of the curtains, which were inspired by Indian sarong fabrics. There is an interesting mixture of textures in the translucent silk curtain panels, the smooth dry cotton of the sofa and ottoman, and the luxurious velvet on the chair and cushions.

The use of pattern on just one swivel chair is inspirational. It is surprising to find a floral print, with its traditional country connotations, on such a modern piece of furniture. The print itself was inspired by an antique fabric from Uzbekistan, but has been given a contemporary spin with this bright orange and blue colourway. Orange is the key to the fresh and stimulating mood – the colour works almost like an appetiser on the palate and gives the other colours a stronger edge. Without these touches of tangerine the room would have a much less invigorating atmosphere, as the other colours are really quite cool. Smaller orange details are woven through the space like a bright thread in the flowers on the table and mugs on the floor.

The design of the furniture follows the industrial feel of the architecture, the graphic lines giving the space an almost masculine feel, but unconventional colours and textures lend the room a lively sensuality. There is a careful balance between straight lines and curves – the clean-cut shapes of the sofa, ottoman and orange chairs, and the sensual curves of the swivel chair and swirling abstract designs on the rug. The modern brushed metal tables are an interesting combination of straight and curved lines, hard and smooth surfaces. Even the flowers are in keeping – tall white arum lilies in simple vases and a single orange hibiscus in a shallow concrete dish.

Blue is considered a peaceful, relaxing colour, but this unusual mixture of bright turquoise and pale ocean with accents of lime and cantaloupe orange is fresh and stimulating. The architecture of this room in a French chateau is extremely formal, and its ornate panelled walls are painted a pale bluish grey (overleaf). To bring contemporary life and spirit to the room, a modern sofa upholstered in bright turquoise bouclé cotton leads the way, with lots of paler blues and white in the other furniture and details. The fabric at the window is the beautiful lily print, this time in turquoise on a crunchy white linen that looks almost translucent with the light shining through it. Under-curtains in a fine modern lace fabric with a leaf pattern add a further layer of luminosity. The partnership of turquoise and lime is most successful – the lime leads the blue and white into a fresher, cooler combination, and is picked up again in the chartreuse cushions and the colour of the foliage in the vases of flowers. Meanwhile, the neutral base of the blue-grey walls is intensified in the pale blues and ocean colours used on the modern ottoman, throws and cushions.

Subtly contrasting textures bring a further note of interest: the bouclé cotton on the sofa, soft washed linen on the ottomans and shiny white plastic for the smaller stools and tables. Most of the shapes lie long and low in this high-ceilinged space, but tall flower arrangements and the two elongated ceramic vases on the table provide a balance for all the horizontals. This is a strong, sophisticated look; the shapes of the furniture are pure and pared-down, the colour palette and use of pattern restrained. For such a minimal style of decorating, however, the mood is unmistakably feminine. Cushions with pretty side bows and ribbon trims just accentuate that mood.

The look and feel of this room could easily be changed with the flowers and cushions alone. With only white flowers, the mood is cool and serene; the addition of a couple of perfect pinky-orange dahlias and just one round cantaloupe cushion brings an element of surprise that's a real tonic for the senses. Unexpected contrasts can heighten one's perception of graphic shapes and patterns – it is touches such as these that bring a real sense of warmth and comfort to the room.

"Who would think that just one cushion could be so important in the creation of a mood? This room would feel quite different without the cantaloupe orange cushion and the fiery orange dahlias on the table. Colour used in this way is very flexible." TG

tricia guild

dynamic colour and dazzling contrasts

A dazzling mixture of contrasting colours and patterns makes this hall a dynamic and welcoming space. A boldly patterned orange print hangs at the tall windows, with wide cuffs of contrasting turquoise and under-curtains in chartreuse and turquoise checked muslin. The sofa is violet, the lamp a vibrant orange, and one armchair is upholstered in bright stripes – offset with an equally colourful flowered cushion. Everywhere you look there is richly concentrated colour. Gazing into this room from another space is like looking into an exciting treasure chest – you can't wait to go in and explore.

The key to using such daring combinations is, as ever, continuity. Often it is the colours of the larger elements in a room, such as a rug or sofa, which hold a room together. Here, it is the striped fabric used in various different colourways on the armchair and cushions. All the colours in the room are to be found in these stripes – the chartreuse at the windows, the persimmon of the curtains, the rich mauve of the sofa – even smaller accents such as flowers, vases, throws and cushions. This subtle colour discipline, along with a conscious repetition of patterns in dynamic diagonals across the space, is what binds the seemingly disparate elements together and enables them to exist in harmony. See how the bold, metallic stencilled fabric of the curtains is used again on the ottomans. The scheme may look free and spontaneous, but it only works because of the care and consideration behind it. The striped cushions have been placed with precision, and even flowers, vases and books have been carefully chosen to knit into the scheme rather than disrupt its balance.

A neutral backdrop plays its part – this combination could not have been assembled in a space with strongly coloured walls or floors. The creamy white walls and pale terracotta floors allow the colours to sing out in all their intensity, and there is a strong white presence in the plain armchair – the perfect foil for its striped neighbour – the leather pouf and contemporary plastic tables. An expanse of the tiled floor is covered with a lighter material that also helps to increase the neutral component in the scheme. Anchoring all the elements is a large square white rug with turquoise and lime borders. This draws all the patterns, shapes and tones together.

"You need a strong anchor to stabilise a daring combination like this. Without the white rug, these contrasting colours and patterns would have been floating in space, but it has the effect of drawing all the elements together onto their own island. This is what gives this large empty space its atmosphere of intimacy. The stripes help blend it together, too, and give it an exciting tension and mixture of graphic shapes." TG

leaves and herbs for summer salads

places to sit in the sun and shade

in the heart of the garden

A walk around this leafy summer garden presents you with a choice of many different places to sit, from the furniture on the terrace near the house to the picturesque old bench and chairs in the shade of the cherry trees. Dip under the leafy arch and you're in the kitchen garden, where another table and stools have been placed in the sun. Nothing is fixed here – a table might be carried into the orchard for a summer lunch, or a bench moved to catch the last rays of the sun one evening. Great fun can be had moving furniture about the garden and creating different scenarios – it's like picnicking with furniture.

"The garden is quite rustic and informal in feel, but the vegetable garden was designed on strong architectural lines, with the different vegetables and flowers confined to their allotted beds. The patterns created by neat rows of salad leaves, zucchini and tomatoes are endlessly satisfying to look at, and clouds of bright flowers grow within separate squares, giving freedom to the geometric space." TG

the satisfying geometry of neat lines of crops

pleasures of picking and gathering for the table

Shot from an upstairs window, the strong architectural design of the kitchen garden can be seen to full effect. There are four entrances, each with an arch entwined with clematis and wisteria, and intersecting paths divide the space into four principal squares. Within each square there are four further divisions, so the different vegetables and flowers arranged in neat blocks and rows are like pieces of a living patchwork quilt. Pink and mauve flowers are concentrated on the side nearest the house, where pots of pink pelargoniums line the steps up from the terrace. On the far side, nasturtiums in every shade from deep red through orange, deep ochre and lemon romp among the vegetables with picturesque abandon. Wonderful large cactus-flowered dahlias are grown in the garden, in stunning shades of deep crimson, scarlet, orange and pink.

dappled sunshine and citrus shades

This is a modern house in the country, and you can really feel the sunshine streaming into this space with its bright citrus shades and leafy patterns. The predominant colour is lime green, accompanied by an interesting mix of turquoise, pale blues, fresh greens and touches of pink. The hard lines of the architecture have been softened by the leaf print at the window – a reference to the trees outside, and the translucent checks in lime and turquoise filter the light and accentuate its sunny, dappled quality. But the geometry of the square-paned windows is too strong to be ignored – it has been picked up in the contemporary prints on the armchair, cushions and ottoman.

"The colours here are harmonious and well-balanced – adding another shade would break the spell.   A chalky soft shade of pink on cushions, floor cushions and on the ottoman print stimulates the other colours, rather than clashing. And lots of white prevents the scheme from cloying. Even the flowers – some luminous creamy dahlias from the garden – are almost exclusively white." TG

"I took the lead for this scheme from the long stylised flowers embroidered on the border of the tablecloth. They have a graphic quality and a modern edge that is accentuated by the matt ceramic plates and tall elegant glasses. Even the lemon tart cut into long thin wedges makes a real impact on the pale blue handmade plates." TG

grapefruit cocktails, an appliqué cloth and slices of fragrant fresh lemon tart

Simple indulgences can be just as enjoyable as more elaborately planned meals – sometimes more so. This table has been laid with a pretty appliqué cloth and pale blue handmade ceramics, and just a few dahlia blooms floated in little cups or scattered on plates. A fragrant lemon tart is drizzled with lemon syrup and cut into slim graphic slices. Prosecco mixed with grapefruit and mango juice in pretty antique glasses is the perfect accompaniment, with the sun shining through the fluted glass. The mood is uplifting, with the scent of fresh lemons hanging in the air.

Designers Guild fabric, wallpaper, upholstery and paint directory

All upholstered furniture by Designers Guild unless otherwise stated

Page 12

Wide Square chairs in Brera Chalk
    F562/15 and Marianao Persimmon
    F1030/04

Curtains in Ribailagua Natural F1033/01

Voiles in Habanera Acacia F1046/03

Wallpaper in Marianao Persimmon
    P378/05

Striped cushions in Lucetas Leaf F1049/02

Walls painted in Chalk

Page 18

Wide Square Chairs in Nurata Ocean
    F1021/14 and in Nurata Geranium
    F1021/09

Edge Stool in Nurata Mango F1021/11

Curtains in Zekh Peony F1013/04 with
    binding in Makasar Acacia F970/09

Voiles in Cozenza Peony F1015/04

Floor cushion in Alacha Crocus F1008/03

Walls painted in Hemp

Page 20

Scoop Sofa in Coba Leaf F1005/08

Curtains in Brera Lapis F562/43 and in
    Brera Chalk F562/15

Walls painted in Cold White and Pale Lime

Page 22

Chill Sofa in Brera Cantaloupe F562/44

Box Chairs in Brera Chartreuse F562/41
    and in Brera Cantaloupe F562/44

Scoop Chair in Brera Chalk F562/15

Chill Stools in Brera Marine F562/40 and
    in Brera Chalk F562/15

Curtains in Brera Crocus F562/46 and in
    Brera Chalk F562/15

Walls painted in Cold White

Page 30

Square Sofas in Lucetas Crocus F1049/04
    with seat cushion in Brera Crocus
    F562/46 and in Lucetas Peony
    F1049/03 with seat cushion in Brera
    Lapis F562/43

Edge Stool in Marianao Ocean F1030/03

Throws on seat cushion in Vitrales Violet
    F1032/03 and in Habanera Aqua
    F1046/02

Curtains in Santovenia Peony F1027/02

Walls painted in Hemp

Page 33

Sleep Sofa in Izapa Magenta F993/02

Scoop Chair in Brera Peony F562/45

Box Chairs in Brera Cantaloupe F562/44
    and in Caracol Peony F997/03

Floor Cushions in Pontalba Cyclamen
    F980/01, in Edzna Magenta F996/02
    and in Tikal Persimmon F994/05

Curtains in Cabildo Schiaparelli F985/02

Voiles in Reticella Persimmon F1000/02
    and in Estrella Cerise F999/02

Rug in Barrisdale Ecru

Walls painted in Chalk

Page 35

Tight Sofa by B&B Italia in Fiesole Clematis
    F968/05

Apta Chair in Brera Chalk F562/15

Striped cushion in Lucetas Crocus
    F1049/04

Voiles in Bise White F942/01

Doors painted in TG Blue

Walls plastered, approximate paint
    colour Dew

Page 38

Elan Sofa by Cappelini in Brera Chalk
    F562/15

Solo Chair by B&B Italia in Fiesole Clematis
    F968/05

Floor cushion in Alacha Peony F1008/01

Voiles in Bise White F942/01

Panelled doors painted in Sea Green

Page 49

Spider Sofa by Cappelini in Brera Chalk
    F562/15

Upholstered cubes in Brera Blossom
    F562/26 and in Brera Chalk F562/15

Walls painted in Borghese Lime

Page 54

Glide Chair by Cappelini in Parioli Verdigris
    F969/07

Floor Cushion in Parioli Aquamarine
    F969/08

Cushions in Parioli Chartreuse F969/09
    and in Khiva Chartreuse F1020/06

Walls painted in Dew

Page 56

Elan Sofa by Cappelini in Brera Ocean
    F562/39

Curtains in Brera Chalk F562/15 with
    binding in Brera Marine F562/40

Page 59

Bed and bedcover in Brera Chalk F562/15

Curtains in Carriaco Ice F921/07

Spring Chaise by Cappelini in Brera Chalk
    F562/15

Throw on bed in Chandeleur Aqua F917/02

Pillows in Brera Marine F562/40

Rug in Barrisdale Ecru

Walls painted in Almond

Page 64

Loop Daybed by Cappelini in Brera Blossom
    F562/26

Curtain in Simoon Petal F938/08

Curtain on bed in Bise White F942/01

Bedcover in Brera Chalk F562/15

Pillows in Brera Blossom F562/26

Throw on bed in Timbalier Blossom
    F918/06

Rug in Barrisdale Ecru

Walls painted in Rose Pink

Page 70

Spider Sofa by Cappelini in Brera Water
    Blue F562/18

Curtains in Callan Natural F619/02

Walls painted in Cold White

Page 77

Solo Sofa by B&B Italia in Safed Silver
    F905/01

Rockford Chair in Gabanti Granite F904/03

Curtains in Timurid Steel F893/04

Cushions in Brera Chalk F562/15, in
    Canareggio Pewter F907/16 and in
    Trovaso Sky F906/05

Walls painted in Ice Blue

Page 79

Bedcover in Safed Peat F905/03

Square pillows in Safed Oatmeal F905/04

Throw on bed in Nakshe Natural F897/05

Curtains in Safed Oatmeal F905/04

Voiles in Batiste Natural F882/01

Walls papered in Nakshe Putty P313/01

Page 80

Elan Sofa by Cappelini in Brera Blossom
F562/26

Solo Chair by B&B Italia in Brera Shell
F562/27

Curtains in Simoon Petal F938/08

Floor cushions in Brera Shell F562/27, in
Brera Chalk F562/15 and in Brera
Crocus F562/46

Page 85

Charles Chair by B&B Italia in Trovaso Pearl
F906/01

Bedcover in Brera Chalk F562/15

Throw in Carriaco Silver F921/02

Curtains in Chandeleur Pearl F917/04

Rug in Barrisdale Ecru

Walls painted in Chalk White

Page 90

Elan Sofa by Cappelini in Fiesole Cyclamen
F968/04

Glide Chair by Cappelini in Parioli Orchid
F969/03

Curtains in Fiesole Clematis F968/05 with
binding in Fiesole Cyclamen F968/04

Cushions in Fiesole Persimmon F968/01
and in Makasar Pale Cyclamen F970/10

Walls painted in Cold White

Page 92

Edge Sofa in Nurata Leaf F1021/12

Edge Chair in Nurata Geranium F1021/09

Curtains in Paranja Leaf F1014/01 with
binding in Sulu Poppy F973/04

Throw in Alacha Peony F1008/01

Rug in Morriston Putty with bindings in
Rouge and Ocean

Walls plastered, approximate paint colours
Hemp and Cold White

Page 98

Loop Daybed by Cappelini in Parioli Bluebell
F969/06

Curtains in Makasar Peony F970/03 and
in Sulu Clematis F973/05

Page 101

Wisconsin Daybed in Sabai Cerise
F974/01

Spider Chair by Cappelini in Fiesole
Persimmon F968/01

Curtains in Puca Damson F960/03 with
binding in Celebes Geranium F972/06
and in Makasar Peony F970/03

Page 104

Escape Sofa in Khiva Cassis F1020/04

Box Chairs in Nurata Peony F1021/08 and
in Nurata Chartreuse F1021/13

Edge Stool in Khiva Chalk F1020/14

Curtains in Nilobi Hyacinth F1011/03 with
binding in Makasar Acacia F970/09

Voiles in Cozenza Hyacinth F1015/03

Page 116

Spring Chairs by Cappelini in Brera Lapis
F562/43, in Brera Cantaloupe
F562/44 and in Brera Mauve F562/04

Walls plastered, approximate paint
colour Lilac

Page 123

Square Sofa in Mahe Hyacinth F466/08

Edge Stool in Khiva Chalk F1020/14

Square Chair in Brera Cyclamen F562/22

Curtains in Pontalba Hyacinth F980/02
  with binding in Sulu Clematis F973/05

Voiles in Cozenza Hyacinth F1015/03

Page 128

Maroushka Metz Chair in Brera Crocus
  F562/46

Curtains in Pitot Lilac F986/03

Bed covered in Brera Chalk F562/15

Throw in Courcelle Lilac F979/01

Walls papered in Pitot Lavender P354/03

Floor painted in Cloud

Page 135

Curtains in Mistral Leaf F939/03

Throw in Carondolet Ocean F983/02

Bedcover in Brera Chalk F562/15

Pillows in Brera Marine F562/40

Floor painted in Cloud

Walls papered in Sakura Turquoise
  P305/01

Page 136

Curtains in La Desirade Lilac F920/02

Bedcover in Brera Chalk F562/15

Throw on bed in Torsello Magenta
  F879/03

Walls papered in Beausejour Lilac
  P323/03

Page 144

Scoop Sofa in Khiva Ocean F1020/08

Scoop Chair in Nurata Mango F1021/11

Chill Stool in Khiva Crocus F1020/11

Sunset Chair by Cappelini in Paranja Cobalt
  F1014/04

Curtains in Rucellai Crocus F1019/05

Walls painted in Chalk White

Page 148

Chill Sofa in Coba Marine F1005/05

Chill Stools in Brera Marine F562/40 and
  in Brera Chalk F562/15

Curtains in Pontalba Azure F980/03 with
  binding in Brera Marine F562/40

Voiles in Merletto Ocean F998/04 and
  Merletto Leaf F998/06

Walls painted in Cloud

Page 157

Edge Sofa in Tejeda Mauve F1048/04

Edge Chairs in Tejeda Chalk F1048/07 and
  in Alfarjes Leaf F1050/01

Edge Stools in Corazon Chartreuse F1031/05
  and in Corazon Ocean F1031/06

Curtains in Corazon Persimmon F1031/02
  with binding in Corazon Ocean F1031/06

Voiles in Yambu Lime F1047/01, Yambu
  Ocean F1047/02, Habanera Aqua
  F1046/02 and Habanera Acacia
  F1046/03

Page 162

Chill Sofa in Tejeda Lime F1048/18

Wide Square Chair in Brera Chalk
  F562/15 with seat cushion in Vitrales
  Blossom F1032/01

Edge Stool in Ribailagua Ocean F1033/03

Curtains in Amarillo Marine F1028/01

Voiles in Yambu Ocean F1047/02 and in
  Yambu Lime F1047/01

Floor Cushion in Vitrales Blossom
  F1032/01

Walls painted in Chalk and Pistachio

Designers Guild stockists

Fabrics, wallpapers, paint, furniture and accessories are available from Designers Guild Homestore 267–277 Kings Road, London SW3 5EN, (020) 7351 5775
and selected retailers including:

bath and n.e.somerset

bristol guild of applied art
68-70 Park Street, Bristol BS1 5JY
0117 926 5548
bristolguild@70parkst.freeserve.co.uk

jane clayton and company
Unit 12 Old Mills, Paulton, Bristol BS39 7SU
01761 412255 enquiries@janeclayton.com

rossiters of bath
38-41 Broad Street, Bath BA1 5LP
01225 462227 rossbath@globalnet.co.uk

berkshire

design village ltd
Silwood Road, Sunninghill, Ascot SL5 0PZ
01344 874487 info@design-village.co.uk

buckinghamshire

john lewis furnishings & leisure
Holmers Farm Way, Cressex Centre,
High Wycombe HP12 4NW
01494 462666

morgan gilder furnishings
14 High Street, Stony Stratford,
Milton Keynes MK11 1AF
01908 568674

cambridgeshire

at home
44 Newnham Road, Cambridge CB3 9EY
01223 321283
postbox@athome-interiors.com

carousel design
1-3 Church Street, St Neots PE19 2BU
01480 211797
carouseldesignco@aol.com

channel islands

voisins department store
King Street, St Helier, Jersey JE4 8NF
01534 870511 c.kempster@voisins.com

cheshire

design emporium
88b Water Lane, Wilmslow SK9 5BB
01625 548771
enquiries@ukdesignemporium.co.uk

john lewis
Wilmslow Road, Cheadle SK8 3BZ
0161 491 4914

cornwall

casa fina interiors
29 River Street, Truro TR1 2SJ
01872 270818
mail@casa-fina.co.uk

devon

fanfare interiors
110 Queen Street, Newton Abbot TQ12 2EU
01626 365428
fanfare2000@hotmail.com

neil bryant interiors
51 Mayflower Street, Plymouth PL1 1QL
01752 667222 enquires@neilbryant.co.uk

sitting rooms
15 Foss Street, Dartmouth TQ6 9DR
01803 834815
sittingrooms@dartmouth96.freeserve.co.uk

sitting rooms
Bickleigh Mill, Bickleigh, Nr Tiverton
EX16 8RG
01884 855722
sittingrooms@dartmouth96.freeserve.co.uk

sitting rooms
62 Fore Street, Totnes TQ9 5RU
01803 865193
sittingrooms@dartmouth96.freeserve.co.uk

dorset

individual interior design
58-60 Poole Road, Westbourne
Bournemouth BH4 9DZ
01202 763256
individual@dial.pipex.co.uk

essex

clement joscelyne
9-11 High Street, Brentwood CM14 4RG
01277 225420
info@clementjoscelyne.co.uk

costello lifestyle
45 Sir Isaacs Walk, Colchester CO1 1JJ
01206 575159

krysia
24 Baddow Road, Chelmsford CM2 0DG
01245 250856 krysiainteriors@aol.com

gloucestershire

upstairs downstairs
19 Rotunda Terrace, Montpellier Street
Cheltenham GL50 1SW
01242 514023
homeclimatesltd@ukgateway.net

hampshire

the interior trading co
55-57 Marmion Road, Southsea PO5 2AT
023 9283 8038
enquiries@interior-trading.co.uk

individual interior design
132 Stockbridge Road, Winchester
SO22 6RN
01962 855165 individual@dial.pipex.co.uk

individual interior design
St Thomas Street, Lymington SO41 9NE
01590 610420 individual@dial.pipex.co.uk

hertfordshire

clement joscelyne
Market Square, Bishop's Stortford
CM23 3XA
01279 506731
info@clementjoscelyne.co.uk

clement joscelyne
111-112 Bancroft, Hitchin SG5 1LT
01462 436533
info@clementjoscelyne.co.uk

david lister interiors
6 Leyton Road, Harpenden AL5 2TL
01582 764270

elizabeth stewart design & furnishing
201-203 High Street, Potters Bar EN6 5DA
01707 663433 esdesign@ukf.net

peter & susan brown
40 Saint Andrew Street, Hertford SG14 1JA
01992 589880

ireland

brian s. nolan ltd
102 Upper Georges Street, Dun Laoghaire
Co Dublin
01 2800564

cotton box design group
Clarinbridge, Galway
091 777040 cbox@interiors.ie

j lyons interiors
Market House, The Square, Castlerea
Co Roscommon
0907 20339

o'mahony interiors
Enniskeane, West Cork
023 47123 o'mahonyinteriors@eircom.net

isle of man

bespoke interiors
92 Strand Street, Douglas IM1 2EP
01624 666310 bespokeinteriors@manx.net

kent

john lewis
Bluewater, Greenhithe, Kent DA9 9SA
01322 624123

kotiki interiors ltd
22-24 Grove Hill Road, Tunbridge Wells
TN1 1RZ
01892 521369 kotikiinteriors@aol.com

mary ensor interiors
37 High Street, Frant, Nr Tunbridge Wells
TN3 9DT
01892 750101 interiors@maryensor.co.uk

mary ensor interiors
13 Crescent Road, Tunbridge Wells TN1 2LU
01892 523003 interiors@maryensor.co.uk

lancashire

john thompson design centre
336 Church Street, Blackpool FY1 3QH
01253 302515

leicestershire

harlequin interiors
11 Loseby Lane, Leicester LE1 5DR
0116 262 0994 harlequinint@aol.com

barkers interiors
94 Main Street, Woodhouse Eaves
Loughborough LE12 8RZ
01509 890473 barkerid@aol.com

lincolnshire

lulu carter design
The Barn, Pulvertoft Hall, Gedney Broadgate
Spalding PE12 0DG
01406 365300
lulufletcher@lulucarter.demon.co.uk

pilgrim decor
2(a) Tawney Street, Boston PE21 6PA
01205 363917

london

charles page interiors ltd
61 Fairfax Road, NW6 4EE
020 7328 9851 info@charlespage.co.uk

the curtain lady and the sofa shop
11-13 Revelstoke Road, SW18 5NJ
020 8947 6225
nickandjacky@thecurtainlady.fsnet.co.uk

designers guild
267 & 277 Kings Road, SW3 5EN
020 7351 5775
uksales@designersguild.com

harrods
87-135 Brompton Road, Knightsbridge
SW1X 7XL
020 7730 1234

heal & son
196 Tottenham Court Road, W1P 9LD
020 7636 1666

john lewis
Oxford Street, W1A 1EX
020 7629 7711

peter jones
Sloane Square, SW1W 8EL
020 7730 3434

interiors of chiswick
454 Chiswick High Road, W4 5TT
020 8994 0073
enquiries@interiorsofchiswick.co.uk

liberty
Regent Street W1 6AH
020 7734 1234

mad cow design
90 Parkhall Road, Dulwich SE21 8BW
020 8761 1008 mad_cow.design@virgin.net

mr jones
175-179 Muswell Hill Broadway, Muswell Hill
N10 3RS
020 8444 6066

selfridges
Oxford Street, W1A 1AB
020 7629 1234

wilson a lifestyle
51 Abbeville Road, Clapham SW4 9JX
020 8675 7775

manchester

orchard interior design
2 Warburton Street, Didsbury Village
M20 6WA
0161 434 6278 orchardinteriors@aol.com

dane
289-291 Deansgate South
0161 834 5831 mail@dane.biz

merseyside

dane
81-83 Bold Street, Liverpool L1 4HF
0151 708 0018 mail@dane.biz

middlesex

interiors with flair
153 St Margarets Road, St Margarets
Twickenham TW1 1RG
020 8255 1001
interiorswithflair@excite.com

norfolk

designers guild at the granary
5 Bedford Street, Norwich NR2 1AL
01603 623220
info@clementjoscelyne.co.uk

northamptonshire

classix design & development ltd
Billing Wharf, Cogenhoe, Northampton
NN7 1NH
01604 891333

northern ireland

beechgrove interiors
53a Loan Road, Cullybackey, Ballymena
Co Antrim BT42 1PS
028 25 880012
sales@beechgroveinteriors.co.uk

fultons fine furnishings
Hawthorne House, Boucher Crescent
Belfast BT12 6HU
0870 600 0186
The Point, Derrychara, Enniskillen BT74 6JF
01365 323739
55-63 Queen Street, Lurgan BT66 8BN
01762 314980

nottinghamshire

nash interiors
60 Derby Road, Nottingham NG1 5FL
0115 941 3811
interiors@nash-interiors.com

alison murday interiors
10a Queen Street, Southwell NG25 0AA
01636 812823 alisonmurday@aol.com

oxfordshire

fairfax interiors
The Old Bakery, High Street, Lower Brailes
nr. Banbury OX15 5HW
01608 685301
caroline.elliott@btconnect.com

stella mannering ltd
2 Woodstock Road, Oxford OX2 6HT
01865 557196
stella@stellamanneringltd.co.uk

scotland

cairns interiors
111 High Street, Old Aberdeen, Aberdeen
AB24 3EN
01224 487490 cairns.interiors@btclick.com

chelsea mclaine interior design
161 Milngavie Road, Bearsden, Glasgow
G61 3DY
0141 942 2833
margot@chelseamclaine.freeserve.co.uk

designworks
38 Gibson Street, Glasgow G12 8NX
0141 339 9520 dwgibsonst@aol.com

john lewis

john lewis
St James Centre, Edinburgh EH1 3SP
0131 556 9121

john lewis
Buchanan Galleries, Glasgow G1 2GF
0141 353 6677

laura gill design ltd
38 High Street, Dunblane FK15 0AD
01786 821948 lauragill@talk21.com

mary maxwell designs
26 Dublin Street, Edinburgh EH1 3PP
0131 557 2173

somerset

paul carter
The Studio, Elm House, Chip Lane, Taunton
TA1 1BZ
01823 330404 thestudio@paulcarter.co.uk

the curtain pole
64 High Street, Glastonbury BA6 9DY
01458 834166 curpole@yahoo.co.uk

suffolk

clement joscelyne
16 Langton Place, Bury St Edmunds
IP33 1NE
01284 753824
info@clementjoscelyne.co.uk

edwards of hadleigh
53 High Street, Hadleigh IP7 5AB
01473 827271
info@edwardsonline.co.uk

grace and mulberry
48-54 Norwich Road, Ipswich IP1 2NJ
01473 287444
info@graceandmulberry.co.uk

surrey

babayan pearce interiors
Braeside House, High Street, Oxshott
KT22 0JP
01372 842437

creative interiors
20 Chipstead Station Parade, Chipstead
CR5 3TE
01737 555443

design studio
39 High Street, Reigate RH2 9AE
01737 248228
enq@the-design-studio.co.uk

heal & son
Tunsgate, Guildford GU1 3QU
01483 576715

heal & son
49-51 Eden Street, Kingston upon Thames
KT1 1BW
020 8614 5900

john lewis
Wood Street, Kingston upon Thames
KT1 1TE
020 8547 3000

j decor interiors
3 South Street, Epsom KT18 7PJ
01372 721773
jdecor@btconnect.com

ochre design ltd
The Old Post Office, 102 High Street, Horsell
Woking GU21 4ST
01483 740222
enquiries@ochredesign.co.uk

sable interiors
7 Criterion Buildings, Portsmouth Road
Thames Ditton KT7 0ST
020 8398 7779

sage
High Street, Ripley GU23 6BB
01483 224396
howard@hsage.freeserve.co.uk

sussex

karin moorhouse interiors
26 High Street, Arundel, West Sussex
BN18 9AB
01903 883653
karin@karinmoorhouse.co.uk

suttons of east grinstead ltd
25-27 High Street, East Grinstead
West Sussex RH19 3AF
01342 321695

suttons furnishings
56 Church Road, Brighton & Hove
East Sussex BN3 2FP
01273 723728

tyne and wear

abercrombies
142 Manor House Road, Jesmond
Newcastle upon Tyne NE2 2NA
0191 281 7182

wales

barrie j knight interior designs
Dennant House, 52 Dew Street
Haverfordwest, Pembrokeshire SA61 1NR
01437 767705
barrie@barrieknightinteriorsfsnet.co.uk

future classics
72 Kimberley Road, Penylan, Cardiff
S. Glamorgan CF23 5DN
029 20 493665

julia jones & co interiors
Conway Road, Mochdre, Colwyn Bay
LL28 5HQ
01492 545013
sales@juliajonesgroup.co.uk

maskreys
116-120 Whitchurch Road, Cardiff
S. Glamorgan CF14 3YL
029 20 229371

warwickshire

fred winter
Guild Street - Henley Street
Stratford-Upon-Avon
CV37 6QY
01789 268011

lee longlands & co ltd
The Regency Arcade, 154-6 The Parade
Leamington Spa CV32 4BQ
01926 438600
lee.leelonglands@leelonglands.com

raisbeck & reason ltd
29 Regent's Street, Leamington Spa
CV32 4SW
01926 889879
info@raisbeckandreason.co.uk

west midlands

john charles interiors
349 Hagley Road, Edgbaston, Birmingham
B17 8DL
0121 420 3977

lee longlands & co ltd
224 Broad Street, Birmingham B15 1AZ
0121 643 9101
lee.leelonglands@leelonglands.com

john lewis
Touchwood, Solihull B91 3RA
0121 709 6841

mary barber fray interior design
222 Alcester Road, Moseley, Birmingham
B13 8EY
0121 4495151

wiltshire

caroline campbell interiors ltd
22-24 Trinity Street, Salisbury SP1 2BD
01722 333222
ccampbellat22@aol.com

worcestershire

cloud nine interiors
12 St Andrews Street, Droitwich Spa
WR9 8DY
01905 779988 cloud9interiors@hotmail.com

yorkshire

homeworks
Charles House, 4 Castlegate, Tickhill
Doncaster DN11 9QU
01302 743978
homeworks@munro.prestel.co.uk

house of elliott
11 Eastgate, Bramhope, Leeds LS16 9AT
0113 284 2960 / 01943 601936

james brindley of harrogate
29-31 James Street, Harrogate HG1 1QY
01423 560757
enquiries@jamesbrindley.com

madelaine peace interiors Ltd
145 Oakbrook Road, Sheffield S11 7EB
0114 230 6666

martin stuart
292-294 Abbeydale Road, Sheffield S7 1FL
0114 258 2462

paper box interiors
141 Wakefield Road, Huddersfield HD5 9AN
01484 546624

plaskitt & plaskitt
59 Monkgate, York YO31 7PB
01904 624670
interiors@plaskittandplaskitt.co.uk

Designers Guild Products are available In
over 40 countries including the following:

argentina

mrs miranda green
Cabello 3919, 1425 Buenos Aires
00 54 1 802 0850

aruba

terra nostra decorations nv
Caya GF Croes 2, PO Box 5080 Oranjestad
00 297 8 30312

australia

**designers guild fabric & wallpaper
(australia)**
Level 1, 79-81 Frenchmans Road
Randwick NSW 2031
00 61 2 9326 5111

linen house (bed & bath)
60 Corporate Drive
Moorabbin VIC 3189
00 61 3 9552 6000

austria

victoria schoeller-szüts
Boersengasse 9/10, A-1010 Wien
00 43 1 535 3075

belgium & luxembourg

acanthus interiors sprl
J.Eerdekensstraat 27, B-3001 Heverlee
00 321 6 292 316

bermuda

howe enterprising!
Po Box HM 3222, Hamilton Hmpx
00 1 441 292 1433

bosnia

entasis
Strosmajerova, 12, 72000 Zenica – BIH
00 387 3241 4633

brazil

formatex representacoes ltda
Rue Oscar Freire, 1119, Sao Paulo
CEP 01426-001
00 11 38 978 130

chile

les tissus
Nueva Costanera 3730, Vitacura Santiago
00 56 2 246 5665

columbia

**denise webb & associates
diseño interior**
Calle 79b # 7-59 Int 4a Bogotà
00 571 255 6194

curaço

the jungle
Lindberghweg #1
00 59 99 465 8640

cyprus

l1 christofides
PO Box 1310, 9 Loukis Akritas Ave, Nicosia
00 357 2 772 939

denmark

lg décor (fabric & wallpaper)
Vejenbrødvej 3, Avderød DK-2980 Kokkedal
00 45 48 28 16 06

zik zak (bed & bath)
Hillerodgade 30A DK-2200 Copenhagen
00 45 35 81 1920

egypt

ebmte
95 A1- Hussein Street, 1st Floor
Midan Al Atebaa, Douki - PO 12411 Cairo
00 20 2 761 7187

finland

verandah
Neitojenpolku 22 D 45, Fin-00810 Helsinki
00 358 9 727 30712

france

designers guild sarl
10 Rue St Nicolas, 75012 Paris
00 331 44 67 80 70

germany

designers guild einrichtuings gmbH
Dreimühlenstrasse 38a, 80469 München
00 49 89 23 11 620

greece

persefone n diamandas & co ee
49 Anagnostopoulou Street Gr-106 73 Athens
00 30 1 361 3810

hong kong

avant garde designs ltd
Shop 133 The Mall Pacific Place 2 88 Queensway
00 852 2 552 7533

hungary

hephaistos haza
Béke Karpitosipari KF7 1056 Budapest
Molnár U 27
00 36 1 266 1550

iceland

vefur
25 Skolavordustig, 101 Reykjavik
00 354 552 2980

indonesia

pt cipta merkurius international
Jalan Abdul Muis No 24-26
Jakarta Pusat 10160
00 62 21 381 0968

israel

ilith
41 Herzel Street, Tel Aviv 66886
00 972 3 683 6716

italy

designers guild srl
Via Masone 2, 24121 Bergamo
00 39 0 35 210 924

japan

mitsui & co ltd
2-1 Ohtemachi 1-Chome Chiyoda-Ku Tokyo 100
00 81 3 3285 1111

kenya

spiegel ltd
First Floor, Esso Plaza, Muthaiga Road
PO Box 38913, Nairobi
00 25 42 762 762

korea

south spring
International Co Ltd, Young Dong, PO Box 344
Seoul 135-603
00 82 2 549 6701

lebanon

perspectives sal
PO Box 4198, Beirut
00 961 1334 120

malaysia

ruffles furnishing
G 6 & 7, Ground Floor, Plaza Ampang
Jalan Tun Razak, 50400 Kuala Lumpur
00 60 3 2142 8573

malta

design house ltd
83 Sir Adrian Dingll Street, Sliema SLM 09
00 35 6 330 855

mexico

artell sa de cv
Calle 20 No 9, Colonia San Pedro De Los Pinos
03800 DF
00 52 5 272 2861

morocco

rodesma textil décor sarl
6 Rond-Point Des Sports, Casablanca
00 21 2 29 72 94

netherlands

wilhelmine van aerssen agenturen
Hoogte Kadijk 143 F2-3, 1018 BH
Amsterdam
00 31 20 640 5060

new zealand

icon textiles ltd
PO Box 9832, Newmarket, Auckland
00 64 9 302 1652

norway

riis interiør as (fabric & wallpaper)
Heggelibakken 2, 0375 Oslo
00 47 22 13 66 80

johns. bjerke as (bed & bath)
PB 9 Slemdal, 0329 Oslo
00 47 22 920 200

phillipines

jody's fabric inc
Unit C, Building 3, 2295 Jannov Plaza
Pason Tamo Extension, Makati City 1231
00 63 2 843 2953

poland

rózne rósnosci sc
Vi Podchorázych 75/77 MI 00-722
Warszawa
00 48 22 841 8815

portugal

pedroso e osório
Rua Fernao Lopes 409-2, 4100 Oporto
00 351 22 616 5030

romania

spazio casa interioare srl
Strada Sfintii Voievozi N.55 – Sector 1
Bucharest
00 40 1 212 31 08

russia

av emme srl
Smolenskij Bul 22, Moscow
00 7 095 937 4230

saudi arabia

ahmed g alesayi
PO Box 5651, Jeddah 21432
00 966 2 669 0071

singapore

**linea tre
(fabric & wallpaper)**
402 Orchard Road, #01-08/10
Delfi Orchard, 238876
00 65 734 554

**CWE Marketing Enterprises
(bed & bath)**
PO Box 81, MacPherson Rd Post Office,
913403
00 65 481 1309

south africa

wellington industries (pty) ltd
Division Home Fabrics,
60 Old Pretoria Road, Halfway House
Midrand, 1685 Johannesburg
00 27 11 266 3700

spain

usera usera
Ayala 56, 28001 Madrid
00 34 9 1 557 94 61

sweden

tapi
Grevgatan 26 NB, S 114 53 Stockholm
00 46 8 661 0380

switzerland

beat haggenmüller
Living Colours, Untergrüt 2
8704 Herrliberg
00 41 1915 5735

taiwan

grc development company if
No 15 Lane 53, Hsin Yi Road
Sec 4 Taipei
00 886 22 752 9740

thailand

sheet'n shade co ltd
344 Rama 3 Road, Bangklo
Bangklorlaem, Bangkok 10120
00 66 2 289 4655-6

turkey

kanape dekorasyon sanayi ve tic. ltd
Kalipci Sok, Uzal Apt. No 152
K:I D:2 – 80200 Tesvikiye Istanbul
00 90 212 241 0365

united arab emirates

aati
PO Box 2623 Dubai UAE
00 971 4 337 7825

usa

osborne & little (fabric & wallpaper)
90 Commerce Road, Stamford
Connecticut 06902
00 1 203 359 1500

westpoint stevens (bed & bath)
20th Floor, 1185 Avenue of the Americas
New York NY 10036 001 212 930 2000

For further information please contact:
Designers Guild
3 Olaf Street, London W11 4BE
tel (0)20 7243 7300 fax (0)20 7243 7333
info@designersguild.com
www.designersguild.com

acknowledgments

My special thanks to our fantastic team who have worked so hard to create this book - Jo Willer, whose contribution is within every page, James Merrell, Elspeth Thompson, Meryl Lloyd and Anne Furniss. Thanks also to Joe Allen, Alain Bernabe, Janice & David Blackburn, Mick Brady, Drew Butler, Myrna Canto, Manuela Caviglione, Marie Christine Caviglione, Julian Cloke, Blythe Evans, Exeter Street Bakery, Tony Flavin, Sylvain Floirac, Liza Grimmond, David Hancock, Mark Homewood, Illy Coffee, Alison & Simon Jeffreys, Tom Keenan, Lisa & Evan Lamberg, Le Mas des Songes, Ralph Levy, Jean-Louis Mennesson, Jacqueline Morabito, Nadia Morellini, Orsino, Angelino Paolino, Richard Polo, Mark Poswillo, Carolyn Quartermaine, Marissa Tuazon, Georgia Wagner, Conroy Winter and the team at Designers Guild.

Editor Anne Furniss

Design Meryl Lloyd

Art Editor Rachel Gibson

Production Nancy Roberts and Vincent Smith

Tricia Guild's Creative Project Manager Jo Willer

All photographs by James Merrell except pages 1, 24-25, 52-53, 74-75, 106-107, 124-125, 152-153, 164-165, 172 by Tricia Guild

First published in 2002 by Quadrille Publishing Limited
Alhambra House, 27-31 Charing Cross Road, London WC2H 0LS

© Photographs James Merrell 2002
© Text Elspeth Thompson 2002
© Design and layout Quadrille Publishing Ltd 2002

British Library Cataloguing in Publication Data
A catalogue record for this book is available from the British Library

ISBN 1 903845 73 4

Printed in Italy